If It Weren't For Eve,
I'd Be A Perfect Wife

By Terri Camp

LOYAL

Loyal Publishing
loyalpublishing.com

If It Were'nt For Eve, I'd Be A Perfect Wife
Copyright © 2002 by Terri Camp
Loyal Publishing, Inc.
P.O. Box 1892, Sisters, OR 97759

Designed by Kent D. Estell
Cover art Copyright © 2002 by Sonya Wilson

ISBN: 1-929125-29-1

Printed in the United States of America

DEDICATION

To Steve, my beloved,

This book is dedicated to you. Without you in my life, I could never have written this book. From the moment we met you have encouraged me to develop my passions and live my dreams. I don't think you quite knew what to think about the dream of having twelve children, yet you still allowed me to dream.

I knew you were supportive of my dream of writing when you decided we "needed" a computer so I could write. Even though the computer was used more for games, my love for writing prospered.

The greatest joy in my life is being best friends with you. I praise God daily for giving me a godly husband and a wonderful father for our children.

I still think you're perfect, even if you still don't call me by my real name.

Your loving wife,
Herb

P.S. I'll make spaghetti next Wednesday.

CONTENTS

ACKNOWLEDGEMENTS

This is the most difficult part of the book to write. It will likely be the least read too. Who reads acknowledgements anyway? Even if no one were to read this page, it must be written. It must be written because tears form in my eyes when I think of all the people who had a hand in my life so that I could write about it.

I'm forever grateful to the Lord for giving me experiences and moments with all of you. Some of the moments I wrote about are painful, and some are joyful. All of them are reasons to give thanks to the Lord. He has woven my life in such a way that I am in this place, at this time, living for Him. He is the only one who truly knows my every thought. And I would sure wish there were times He would whisper some of those thoughts to my husband, Steve.

There are so many times I wished that Steve would read my mind. And there were times that I was certain he could. Life would not be complete for me without the love of you in my life.

Steve brought with him several people into my life when we met. Among those I would especially like to thank are Mom and Dad Camp. Your love and ability to embrace me as a daughter of your own have enriched my life beyond what you can even imagine. Thank you for all of your encouragement and for raising a son who would later become my husband. If my boys grow up to be like their father, I will owe much of that to you.

To my parents and my sister I would like to say you have been with me through it all. You experienced my rebellion first hand. You experienced my pain. I caused you all many tears in your life, but you always stayed by me, praying for me, and loving me unconditionally. Dad, I want to especially thank you for having the courage to speak the truth to me when I especially needed it. My hope is that I have also been able to bring you all much joy.

To my children I want to simply say, "Thank you for making my life complete."

INTRODUCTION: IF IT WEREN'T FOR EVE

Have you ever been even a little bit irritated when you think of Eve eating the forbidden fruit? Frankly, I sometimes get downright upset with that woman. It's a good thing I will never run into her in the produce aisle at my grocery store. I might be tempted to throw something at her—like an apple.

Think about this for a minute. Eve was married to the most handsome man on the face of the earth. She didn't worry about her hair, or, for that matter, even her clothes. There was no laundry to do. She didn't have to cook. All she had to do, all day long, was talk to the animals, talk to her husband, and talk to her Lord. This woman was in paradise! And if she didn't want to talk, she could admire the beauty of her garden, where there was never a weed in sight. She could eat fruit from almost any tree she wanted. She could even lie down next to a lion. Haven't you always wanted to do that? I have.

This woman had it made.

Then, one day, while taking her afternoon stroll through that wonderful garden, she happened on a crafty dude. Clearly, the serpent forgot to tell Eve, when he was explaining how great it would be for her to eat from the tree of the knowledge of good and evil, that with it would come horrible infirmities, like laundry, dirty dishes, and PAIN. Not to mention the part about wanting to rule over her husband.

Oh no, this crafty creature did not tell her how difficult it was going to be when her husband told her, "We can't afford a new front-loading washing machine." He did not tell her that her entire being would want to shout at him, "But I *want* one!"

No, the serpent was ever so sly. He convinced Eve that the fruit was irresistibly delicious. He failed to mention that her eating it would condemn all women, for the rest of time, to slaving over hot stoves. And to having children in pain, after which they would end up with stretch marks, wrinkles, and fat.

If only Eve had not eaten the fruit. We would still be enjoying our strolls in the evening, instead of doing dishes after dinner. We would still enjoy the thought of childbirth. We would not need new front-loading washing machines. Indeed, we would not even feel the need to tell our husbands what we really think of their decisions.

We would be perfect wives.

PART ONE:
WHO'S IN CHARGE HERE, ANYWAY?

1
I Saw Him First!

Steve always claims that he saw me first. But I'm absolutely certain it was the other way round.

We were both in the Air Force. I was at the lowest point in my life when I first set eyes on him. I had gone out with a man I barely knew, and ended up being raped by him and several others. I was left feeling helpless and abused, but also an idiot, stupid and naïve. I was searching for something in my life, but I didn't know what. The word "hope" was not a part of my vocabulary.

From my early teens, I had been on a constant search for love and acceptance. It still brings tears to my eyes when I think how, instead of looking right in front of me, at the ones who loved me most, I kept searching for love in people who didn't care about me at all.

How I hurt my parents by my irresponsible behavior! Each time I phoned them, it was with yet another tale of woe. Talking to my dad the day after I was raped, he said, "Sometimes you have to purpose in your life that you will no longer be a victim, but that you are going to be a success." They were the most painful, but also the most loving words he ever said. They made my eyes sting again with tears. But they also put into my heart a new resolve to change my life.

That night, I decided that I was not going to be a victim of myself again. A time of healing my life began. I found new confidence. And I realized that, when I set my mind on something, I was going to succeed.

One of the first attempts I made at healing my life was to begin attending group counseling sessions, after admitting to my Senior Officer that I used marijuana. Little did I know what a profound impact those sessions were going to have on my future.

When I walked in the door for the first session, with a fellow Airman who had been caught drunk, my eyes immediately zeroed in on a handsome young man in an officer's uniform. Lieutenant Steve Camp. And my heart skipped a beat. My cheeks flushed and I quickly looked away as our eyes met.

Proof positive. I did see him first.

I don't remember any of that counseling session. I kept feeling drawn to this man in blue. I stole glances at him every chance I got.

A couple of nights before, I had fallen off my top bunk at the barracks where I lived, and was hobbling about on crutches. Passing by Lieutenant Camp at the break, to go outside for a cigarette, I tripped on something and practically landed in his arms. Purely accidental, of course. He had to help me up. That did it. I was definitely hooked.

Walking to the parking lot with a friend after the session, I saw Steve get into his car. I told my friend, "I'm going to marry that man."

Steve and I ended up being in the same small group meetings. I knew this was a sign from God. Even though I wasn't familiar with God, I was certain that He was speaking to me. I had found myself praying for the pain in my life to end. I knew of the God who was spoken of in the church that I went to occasionally as a child.

I often turned to Him when I was in trouble, but I don't recall ever asking Him to direct my life. I knew enough about Him, though, that when I saw that Steve was in the same group as I was, I felt that it was a "God thing."

For four weeks in that small group I barely spoke a word. We were there to "share," and I was painfully shy about expressing my true feelings. But in my mind, I was saying to Steve, "Marry me! Marry me! You really want to marry me!"

Each week, I unearthed more information about this man I was destined to marry. Of course, he was still clueless about the matter. As the fifth week began, I realized that, if I was going to marry him, I first had to get his attention. And I only had one more week to do it before the group sessions ended. I had a plan, which I set out to fulfill, of marrying this handsome officer and gentleman.

I learned that it would be considered fraternization if I dated an officer, but it wasn't fraternization to marry one. So I thought perhaps getting married right away was probably the best course of action. I just had to get him to propose. A minor detail.

One day, after seeking wisdom from others, I decided to send Steve an anonymous letter attached to a flower. Of course, if I were going to ask someone to marry me, it would be better if he actually knew who I was. I could not make the letter totally and completely anonymous. I decided to write the letter in a different language. My plan was to write the letter using a translation dictionary. Then, I would hide out at the library and wait for my prince to come in to decipher his letter.

I wrote several drafts. The first was right to the point. I said, "It's against the rules for an officer to date enlisted personnel, so let's just get married." No. That was a little too straightforward. Instead, I opted for some explanation. "Dear Sir," I wrote (that is proper Air Force etiquette). "I have been watching you for some time and would like to get together with you for some intellectual stimulation. You may phone me at this number after four thirty." I signed it, "Your Monday and Wednesday afternoon admirer."

At the library, I checked out an English-Italian dictionary, and set about translating my letter word for word. The following day, I went to the florist and ordered a peach rose to send with it.

All day I was on pins and needles. What if he wasn't able to figure out who I was? What if he didn't want anything to do with me? What if I had really made a fool of myself?

Apparently I didn't function at work very well that day. My boss came in and let me go home half an hour early.

At exactly four thirty, the phone in our dorm bathroom rang. I didn't expect it to be him, so I answered rather nonchalantly. When he asked for me, Airman Sween, I knew it was him. My heart began to race faster. I didn't know what to do. I said, "Just a minute, please."

"Wait," he said. "Could you tell me her first name?"

"Terri," I said. I put the phone down and went into my dorm room. When I told my roommate who was on the phone, we screamed together. She then had to remind me that I should actually go back to the phone to talk to my Prince Charming. I wondered how I was going to be able to tell this man that I really didn't need to get to know him. I just needed to marry him.

Again, I opted not to be so straightforward. I went back to the phone and said, in the calmest voice I could muster while my heart was leaping out of my chest, "Hello?" We talked that night for a couple of hours. He told me that his barber is Italian so he had taken my note to him to translate. Of course, the Italian barber knew it had not been written by anyone who knew Italian! We set a date for the following Friday.

The next night he called me again, and we talked for several hours. I could barely wait for the night to come when I would be able to meet him without several watchful eyes. When the day of our date finally arrived, I was surprised by the delivery of a dozen red roses. Attached to them was a poem written in Spanish. I had my first sergeant translate it. As he read, he interrupted himself to say, "Who is this joker?" But I know that, secretly, he felt this "joker" was a decent human being.

Finally, the day arrived. Lieutenant Camp became known to me as Steve. He came to my door, and walked with me to his car. He went to my door and opened it for me. I knew by that simple gesture that he was the prince I had been waiting for. Instead of riding on a white horse, he came in a red Honda.

I got in and rode off into the sunset with my prince.

2
Imperfectly Charming

Even though I had met my "prince," I still felt at times my life was spiraling downwards. I had to be a witness at the trials of the men who raped me. Each time that I was called to testify and remember that night, I relived the pain. There was more pain than just the memory; there was the pain of knowing that I had been failing in my life. I felt hopeless.

Around this time, I reached a point when I wanted to be done with life. It only seemed to bring me pain. Driving home one afternoon from testifying, I decided that I would rather not live any longer. I put a tape in my tape player, turned it up as loud as I could, and began to accelerate rapidly. As my car drew closer to the edge of no turning back, a phrase on the tape stuck in my head.

The tape was by a Christian singer named Steve Camp. My sister had sent it to me when she discovered I was dating a man named Steve Camp. As the rhythm pounded in my head and pulsated through my body, the words haunted me. The song spoke of hope and of a God that cares for us all. Quickly I slammed on the brakes. I was seconds from flying off the end of the road. But the Lord came and ministered to me. I knew that I was changed at that moment. I felt hope for the first time in a long time. I knew I would get through the next few trials. I knew there was a God.

Never in my life before had I known such kindness as Steve showed to me. We soon became inseparable. When I shared with Steve the pain that stared me in the face every night as I returned to my barracks, just across the basketball court from the men who had hurt me, he invited me to live with him in his apartment. I jumped at the idea of not having to see those men each day.

When Steve did propose to me, it was not in the way I had planned.

I was lying in a hospital bed with an I.V. in my arm and my face swollen so large I could barely move my lips to talk. I had an abscessed tooth that had spread infection into my bloodstream. I had gone to the hospital late at night, when I awoke in awful pain and then saw my swollen face in the mirror. The dentist told me that I could have been dead by morning, as the infection was spreading rapidly through my system.

When Steve came in to see me, he bent down to kiss me, and all I could say was "ouch!" As he sat near me, tears came into his eyes. He talked about how scared he was that he might lose me. Then he told me that he was certain he wanted to spend the rest of his life with me. It wasn't exactly the marriage proposal I had envisioned. On the outside, I could barely muster a smile. Still, on the inside, I was leaping for joy.

You could say Steve had a captive audience. He talked of his dream of us getting married on the fourth of July. He wanted always to have the day of our anniversary off, and to have fireworks. Then, no matter how dull our marriage got, we would always have fireworks on our anniversary. Quite the romantic, he was.

Once recovered, I began to plan for the wedding. For some reason, I was drawn to a Christian bookstore for wedding information, even though Steve and I did not go to church at all. I grew up in a Lutheran church and, though I sometimes cried out to Jesus when things in my life were really going bad, religion was not part of my day-to-day life. Steve was raised in an Episcopal Church, and went to church every Sunday as a child. When we met, he wanted nothing to do with religion. He was fairly certain that there wasn't a God anyway, so he didn't see the point.

This was just one of our many differences.

It didn't take me too long to figure out that, even though I was madly in love with my prince, he wasn't all perfectly charming. He did have a few quirks. For one thing, he looked great in his uniform but, when he got home from work, he always changed into truly strange-looking clothes. My first order of business was to take him shopping. But for some reason, whenever we went out, he still wanted to wear his silly red high-top tennis shoes, Air Force-issue shorts, t-shirt and tube socks. Why didn't he want to wear the great clothes I had picked out for him? After all, he paid for them.

Oh well, I thought. I could certainly overlook this, even the red high tops. At least for a while. I was certain that I would be able to change him.

Steve also lacked an appreciation for spontaneity, which I thrived on. I would come home from work and say, "Let's go get some pizza. In Los Angeles."

His response? "But that's two hours away!"

At first, he went with me anyway. But not before packing an ice chest with soda pop for the drive down and back. I thought that was ridiculous. Isn't that what gas stations are for? Once, as I tried to rush him out the door, he finally said to me, "Do you know how much money we save by packing our own drinks?" Of course I didn't. Why would I think about such trivial matters as money? Which may have explained why he had a lot and I had none.

My attitude was that you spent what money you had, and then you were done spending it. He thought you needed to save money. Of course, with me around, he didn't get to do a lot of saving. At first, I think he really enjoyed taking me places and spending money on me. But eventually he just wanted to stick around his place and watch movies.

That was another thing we didn't agree on. I wasn't a big fan of movies, unless they were sappy love stories. He was a James Bond man. I thought James Bond was a wimp. I liked to watch sitcoms. He didn't. I liked to listen to love songs on the radio. He liked weird music.

Steve wasn't a big fan of change. I thrive on change. I love to rearrange the furniture. He likes to sit in his chair in the place that his chair belongs. He thinks it's frivolous to make scale drawings and try to figure out the best placement of furniture, only to do it again a couple of weeks later.

All of these disagreements were minor, though. He was my prince, and eventually the prince always changes into what the princess wants him to be. I was certain that, the more time we spent together, the more he would realize that my way was the right way to do things.

I was also certain I would be able to conquer the difference in our attitude to religion. I even convinced Steve that we should go to church. So we went…once. But I hungered for the hope and the peace that I had once felt. That is why my search for wedding information took me to a Christian bookstore. I bought a book on marriage and a record (remember those big round vinyl things?) of wedding songs. But, as I planned our fourth of July wedding, the realization came that perhaps the wedding should be moved up.

When the doctor called to tell me that I was indeed pregnant, I was unsure how I felt. I did not want to get married because I was pregnant. I didn't want Steve to feel "trapped" by me.

My fears were unfounded. When I told Steve about the baby, he was very excited. We got married on New Year's Eve instead—and still had fireworks. To be honest though, I think I would have seen fireworks no matter what day we were married.

Even though we didn't enter into our marriage exactly the way I would have planned, I was determined that I was going to be the perfect wife.

3
Desire? What's That?

"To the woman He said: 'I will greatly multiply your sorrow and your conception; In pain you shall bring forth children; Your desire shall be for your husband, And he shall rule over you'" (Genesis 3:16).

A friend once sent me a pad of post-it notes that pictured a hen sitting on a pile of about forty eggs. The caption read: "Motherhood is not for wimps."

Isn't that the truth! I can't think of anything more difficult than being a mother. We begin by consuming—and trying to keep down—more saltine crackers than any other substance known to man. From there, the difficulties are only magnified.

The day before our firstborn, Ashley, came into the world, I experienced my first California earthquake. I was lying asleep in our waterbed when something like a herd of elephants shook the roof and our dog jumped all over me. The waves nearly tossed me to the floor. Next to the bed the empty cradle, waiting for my unborn child, was rocking like crazy. I believe it may have been a sign from God of what was to come.

Shortly after Ashley was born, I heard Steve say to his brother on the other end of the phone, "It was no problem at all."

I thought to myself, *"No problem at all? I feel like I was run over by a Mack truck!"*

I was not a Christian then, but I still knew it was Eve's fault that the Mack truck ran over me several times.

Then, I looked at my beautiful baby and I knew I would gladly be run over for her. I remember hearing a woman say that, as soon as you have a baby, your heart suddenly walks around outside of your body. That was how I felt. The first time your child cries and you don't know why, your heart breaks. Terror strikes every time you think something may be wrong with your precious baby. Everything she does is scrutinized. Every wrong she commits becomes a mom's personal sorrow. There is no way around this.

One day when Ashley was about three weeks old, she slept for four hours straight. She was still breathing. I know because I checked her every fifteen minutes. Finally, I called our doctor's office. "The problem," I said, "is that my baby is asleep, and has been for a long time."

I'm sure the nurse thought I was nuts. She said, "When was the last time you had a good soak in the tub?"

I took the hint and ran a bath. Of course, just as I put in my big toe to test the temperature of the water, my precious baby woke up. And I groaned. But when I went in to pick her up, I decided I would gladly give up my bath to be with her.

Yes, I would gladly give up anything for her.

I wish I could say I felt that way about Steve.

The part in the verse above that says "Your desire shall be for your husband" always perplexed me. It didn't make sense that this should be part of the curse. Isn't the sexual relationship with your spouse supposed to enhance a marriage? Why would desire for my husband be part of the curse?

Somehow, as soon as our first baby was born, I missed out on that part of the curse anyway.

Desire was not something I even thought about. If Steve made moves towards me, I secretly hoped that the baby would wake up.

Sure, there were times when I desired my husband. Mostly, though, I was too tired even to think about giving anything more when it was time for bed.

One night, as I was once again telling Steve, "No, I'm tired," he retorted that he wanted to clone me. He said there wasn't enough of me to go around, and it would be better for him if he had a second me for bedtime.

I found it encouraging that he thought two of me would be better than one.

The trouble was that, by the time Steve got home from work, my original body was ready to call it quits for the day. And there was still so much to do—dinner, cleaning up, bathing the kids. By the time they were in bed, I was too exhausted to do more than slump into a chair. I had nothing left over to give Steve.

Yet, as I looked around the house, there was no evidence of all I had done. I might not have lifted a finger all day long. You couldn't see the countless kisses that had made bangs and falls and wounded hearts feel better. You couldn't see the results of an hour's play in the park, of Mom trying to swing two children while making sure that the one-year-old didn't go flying down the tornado slide headfirst at lightning speed. A mom has nothing tangible to show at the end of a day when she ran around the merry-go-round three hundred and sixty times. No one can see that she had children sitting in her lap, crawling on her back for piggyback rides, kissing, hugging, and touching her all day. Nothing on the outside indicates the time she spent coloring, or dancing and singing with The Donut Man.

I discovered early in my parenting how utterly exhausting even just two little children can be. I had been feeling nauseous for several weeks—for the usual reason. Well, at last I reached the triumphal second trimester of pregnancy, and I was ready to get things back under control. Actually, I doubt if I ever did have things under control, but I like to think I might have.

On Day One of the second trimester, I arose early in anticipation of a new me. Aha! Just as I suspected—I had energy again. And no more need for saltines.

I began that morning by looking through the house to see what damage had occurred in the previous three months. Everything was a mess. Floors needed mopping, furniture needed vacuuming, dishes were piled high in the sink. And the bathroom well, the less said about that the better.

To battle! My first plan of action was to mop the kitchen floor, a job best tackled while my two munchkins were still asleep.

I finished mopping just as the girls woke up. After the morning routine of changing, washing, brushing and hugging them, I sat them down for their morning cereal. Then, on to the living room to begin vacuuming.

Even over the sound of a vacuum, I heard the giggling, and the CRASH that followed. I looked into the kitchen just as Christi was hurling her cup of juice across the room to join the two bowls of cereal already lying face down on my freshly cleaned floor.

I mopped the floor again.

Just as I was doing the final rinse, I heard another terrible CRASH, followed by a loud cry. At the speed of Mom (much faster than Superman), I flew into the living room. Apparently, Christi had tried to climb the mantle, using my spider plant as her rope. The plant now lay at her feet, along with the broken pot and all the potting soil.

I vacuumed the living room again.

All quiet. I turned the television on to Sesame Street for them, and went to clean the bathroom. After scrubbing the tub, I checked back in on the girls.

They weren't in the living room.

There was no sign of them anywhere in the house.

I went out the front door. Still no one. Panic began to set in. I ran out the back door. As I called and called, I finally heard Ashley's piping voice. "Here we are. Christi and I are taking a bath." I turned the corner of the house to find my girls covered from head to toe in sand. I dusted them off and carried them through the kitchen, over the newly mopped floor, through the living room, dropping sand on the freshly vacuumed carpet, and deposited them in the clean bathtub.

After bathing them, I collapsed, exhausted, into a chair. My second trimester triumph was going to have to wait until another day. Then I glanced at the clock. It was nine thirty. In the morning.

I had been up for two hours. I had mopped the kitchen floor twice, vacuumed the living room twice, and cleaned the bathtub, twice. And none of those things looked like they had been done. It was no wonder my husband often walked into the house, saw me sitting in the chair, and asked, "What have you done all day?"

When the kids were finally asleep, romance was the last thought on my mind. I was kissed and hugged out. I didn't have anything physical left to give. When eleven o'clock rolled around, all I wanted was to roll over and sleep.

Not Steve. He had a desk job. For him, it was time to get physical!

When I think about it, it is sad that my husband always had to try to convince me we should have sex. For many years, I looked at sex as a chore, as something to be submitted to and endured, rather than enjoyed.

Steve often tried to convince me with favorite lines, such as, "You'll like it." And I did like it. But it didn't seem worth the effort that I had to go through. I found myself getting resentful toward Steve. I cringed when I saw that look in his eye, or if he touched me a certain way that meant, "I want you." At those moments, I would rather have been anywhere in the world than in bed with him.

I struggled with this area of our married life for years. Everything seemed to become rooted in the sex part of our marriage. If we went out together, I knew it meant that, later, I would have to "perform." I could not cuddle with Steve without thinking I would have to do something more. And so I began to withdraw from him.

I couldn't believe how much time I spent thinking about not wanting to make love to my husband. So much of what I did was governed by how "frisky" it would make Steve, and whether or not I was going to "feel like it" when the time came.

And, night after night, I said "no."

Occasionally, I felt an obligation to please my husband, and so I would submit to having sex. Even then, Steve's biggest gripe was that I never initiated any of our "romantic" times. He wanted me to wear skimpy, sexy things. I wanted to wear sweats. How could I initiate what I considered to be a dreaded chore?

It irritated me when Steve reminded me of how many days it had been since we were "together." I knew. That didn't make me feel any better about the whole idea. I did not want to perform for the sake of performance.

I loved my husband. That wasn't the issue. My problem was that love and sex were not even on the same page in my book. I figured I could have the one without the other.

Over the years I grew more distant from Steve, thinking that would make him want me less. But even when I was cold to him, it didn't make any difference.

One day, after several years of living in this cold, distant mode, I knew that I did not want to be in that place any longer. I wanted our relationship to change. Which meant I had to ask the Lord to change me.

This was difficult. I first had to work up the courage to be able to tell the Lord. Did I think that He didn't already know?

In thinking about my problem, I came to a devastating realization. Everyone I had ever slept with, before Steve and I were married, was haunting me when Steve and I came together. I had never asked God to forgive me, and I had never forgiven myself. If I were going to have the best relationship possible with Steve, I would have to put my past where it belonged—behind me, and buried forever.

One of the hauntings of my past was the multiple rape that occurred when I was in the Air Force, shortly before Steve and I met. The women's barracks was separated from the men's only by the length of a basketball court. I was an extremely promiscuous young woman and, one day, sunbathing on the court in a bikini, I flirted with a member of the Security Police. We made a date to see each other later on.

I had several drinks before I followed this man to his room that night. Unless I was drunk, it was difficult for me to have sex with someone I barely knew.

Time, and everything around me, became fuzzy. Several hours later, I realized that we were not alone. The room was full of men, each of them taking their turn with me. At first I was too drunk to fight, but the realization of what was happening sobered me up. I began to sob. One of the guys took pity on me and threw me out the door.

Even now, this memory causes me much agony.

Many times, in intimate moments with Steve, I suddenly felt transported back in time, and felt helpless and abused again. It had nothing to do with Steve. For some reason, I was too ashamed to tell him I was haunted by these terrible thoughts from my past.

Finally, one night, when I was alone in my car coming back from a Mom's Night Out, the Lord met with me. He often rides in my car with me. As I drove and talked to the Lord, He convicted me that there were many issues that I had to come to terms with. It was time for me to take responsibility for my part in the whole thing.

I cried and cried as I drove down the road, reliving what had been a night of terror. But it was so comforting to know the Lord was with me, leading me by the hand as I experienced that moment again.

I saw something almost unbearably painful. I saw a woman who was not completely innocent. I saw a woman who had perhaps encouraged the event to happen. It's not that I believe rape is an issue of sex. But, as with anything that happens in life, I do think there are times we must take responsibility for our part. In this case, I had to come to terms with that.

Early on in the investigation that followed the incident, I had been told that none of it was my fault. So I buried the thought of anything that would have been my responsibility. But when you bury sin, it comes back to haunt you. Only God can bury our sin, after we have confessed it, and repented.

My sin had haunted me all those years. As the Lord walked with me that night in my car, I was able to see what I needed to confess. I needed to confess that I was the one who had initiated the idea of visiting the room of a man I barely knew. I needed to confess that I was not sinless throughout the whole ordeal. I confessed to God all the areas that He painfully revealed to me.

But there was still more to do. I had to confess to Steve. He had to know, or I would never be free.

I arrived home well past two in the morning. The last thing I wanted to do was wake my husband to confess my sin to him. So I gave the Lord a condition. (This is NOT a good idea). I told the Lord that I would not wake Steve up. If I found Steve asleep, I would tell him the next day.

Even as I made this condition, I knew that, if I waited, I might lose my nerve.

I'm sure you can guess what happened. I removed my shoes, all the more quietly to slip into our room. Steve sat up immediately and said, "I was getting worried about you."

A flood of tears poured down my cheeks. I confessed to him. I really had it in my mind that, once Steve knew what a horrible person I was, he would consider it the last straw. I was sure that he would pack up our kids and go off to find someone worthy to be their mom.

Far from it.

Steve had thought I was lying dead in a ditch somewhere. He was relieved to discover I was just a poor wretched sinner.

He took me in his arms, wiped away my tears, and promptly fell asleep.

It was a confession that changed my life. No more was I haunted by unrepented sin. No more did I cringe when Steve touched me. No more was I tired at night.

Wait! That's not true. I still haven't figured out how not to get worn out during the day. Maybe I really should be cloned. Then one of me can do all the hard stuff like being a mom. And the other one can do the fun stuff, like desiring my husband.

But wait again. There's more. "Your desire shall be for your husband, And he shall rule over you." Who put that part in there?

4
Not Him, Lord!

Ten days after the birth of our second daughter, I hemorrhaged at home, and was sent to the hospital for a D & C, to remove some retained placenta. My doctor told us, prior to the surgery, that it would take about an hour and I would be home by midnight.

That wasn't exactly how it worked out. The surgery took several hours. I even woke up on the operating table, which was by far one of the most frightening experiences of my life. I felt complete helplessness.

As I came to again in the recovery room, I was informed that I had lost a lot of blood, prior to and during the surgery. Nurses checked on me constantly, pressing my fingernails and toenails to check my circulation. My blood pressure was critically low. I whispered to Steve to call my dad. I wanted him to call my sister to pray for me. I wasn't certain that I was going to survive.

The following day, the male nurse who had been with me right after the surgery told me he was surprised that I had made it. He even told me that he and his wife, who was a nurse in the emergency room when I was there, went home and prayed for me. This really had a big impact on me. I didn't know of people, other than relatives, who were willing to pray for a perfect stranger. I wonder now, after all these years, what they prayed for. Did they pray for healing? Did they pray for salvation? What did the Lord prompt them to say while they were on their knees that night?

Whatever it was, their prayers were answered.

After several blood transfusions, and three days in the hospital, I was finally able to go home to my new daughter, Christi, and her older sister, Ashley. But something was different in me.

Even though I knew of Jesus, I was by no stretch of the imagination walking with Him as my Lord and Savior. But somehow, I knew that I needed Him right then. I had a desire to go to church. I began attending a Bible study at the invitation of the wife of one of Steve's colleagues. Later, I started going to the church to which several of the ladies at the Bible study belonged.

Steve didn't want to go to church with me. He was an agnostic. In truth, he felt that he'd had enough of church as a kid. He went to church every Sunday, and was even an altar boy. He was pretty much churched out, and didn't see the point. So, I went with my two little ones, without Steve.

One day, the pastor asked if there was anyone who needed to ask the Lord into his or her heart. My hand shot up. I didn't feel changed, but I felt an incredible desire to read a Bible. Isn't it amazing how we don't necessarily see the change, but we are changed dramatically?

The women at the Bible study helped and encouraged me in my new Christian walk. Even though Steve was not saved, they also encouraged me to win him with my actions, not with my words.

My desire to read the Bible was so strong that I read it during virtually every waking moment. After a while, Steve told me that I was ruining our marriage. "We had a perfectly good marriage," he said, "until you went and got religious on me."

I continued to read. Every once in a while, I tried to share with him some of the interesting things I was reading, but he didn't want to hear. He wanted his old wife back, the one who was happy to do nothing but veg out in front of the television with him.

Each Sunday, I asked Steve if he wanted to go to church with me. For about five months, his answer was always, "No!" Then, one day, he said, "Sure, I'll go."

He actually enjoyed himself, and enjoyed getting to know some of the people there. One day, I was watching the 700 Club on TV and I saw Steve bow his head and pray with Pat Robertson. "WOW!" I thought. "That's cool!"

Later that week, the pastor of the church dropped by to talk with Steve. He shared with him some verses from the Bible. I was shocked that Steve did not even know John 3:16. How could he have gone to church week after week and have missed that basic truth? "For God so loved the world that He gave His only begotten Son, that whoever believes in Him should not perish but have everlasting life." That was the whole point of it all.

The pastor shared many verses with Steve that day: "...for all have sinned and fall short of the glory of God" (Romans 3:23), and: "But God demonstrates His own love toward us, in that while we were still sinners, Christ died for us" (Romans 5:8).

Afterward, Steve said he would like to pray with our pastor. He knew he needed a Savior, and needed to be forgiven for his sins. However, he confessed to me later that he wasn't sure that he was entirely honest and trusting in his heart at that point.

Even though Steve didn't feel changed, I could tell that he was different. He began to question me about the Bible. He thought I was now the authority on it. And, apparently, I thought so too.

Soon afterwards, as we lay in bed talking about spiritual things, we both sensed a sudden presence in our room. It nearly paralyzed Steve. I could sense that it was an evil presence, and felt goose bumps all over me. Steve grabbed my hand and said, "Let's pray. *Right now!*" For the first time, I heard him pray with conviction.

The presence left us immediately. Later, Steve said that he had felt he was going to die. The evil presence, which I had felt mildly, he felt on top of him, daring him to choose Jesus. And he chose. He lay awake thinking about it almost the rest of the night.

That was the turning point in Steve's life. I was certain that he was saved. But you know what? I still wanted to be the spiritual leader in our home. I looked at him and thought, "He can't be the spiritual leader. He has sin in his life." As if I didn't? But apparently I didn't see my own sin. So I continued on the leadership path in our family. When we moved, I chose the church. When we were invited to a parenting class, I said yes. Everything that was spiritual was *mine*. And I was more than willing to accept the responsibility.

Steve went to the church I had chosen. But he began to find reasons to not go every Sunday. This, of course, fueled my desire to continue as the spiritual head of our home. After all, I was certain God's word said that only "good enough" men were to lead in their homes. If the women were better, then certainly God would want them to be the leaders.

After a year or so at our new church, we were invited to a parenting class the church was hosting. I took the invitation to mean that the person who invited us thought we really needed to get our children in order. I didn't want to be known in church as having unruly children, so *I* decided we would attend.

I begged Steve to go with me. After attending three of the classes, he decided that he didn't want us to go anymore.

What? How could he make such a decision? This was a *parenting* class. We were *parents*. We *had* to go to the class. We had to learn how to be good parents! But he thought we already were good parents. He didn't want our children's every waking moment scheduled. And he certainly didn't think it was necessary for them to have their childhood ruled by an iron fist. So he informed me, impolitely, that we were not going to attend the class anymore.

I was furious.

I decided that, if Steve didn't want to help our children by learning to be a better parent, then I would go to the classes by myself. I would be the best parent. So I went the next night, alone. I came home and informed Steve about all the things we were doing wrong. But he didn't want to hear it.

I decided that I wouldn't go again.

I didn't let Steve decide. I decided. I thought I had better pray for Steve. He really needed to learn the benefits of attending parenting classes. So I prayed.

This parenting class thing bothered me for a long time. Whenever I thought Steve was handling the kids wrong, I thought to myself, "See. He should have taken that course." I equated his behavior with that of a doctor who only attended a few of the lectures on how to perform brain surgery, but still thought he was capable of operating.

I held a grudge about this matter for years. Every time I heard about the same course being offered, I wanted to go. Finally, I decided that I should try to get him to take a different parenting course with me.

No go.

I thought perhaps I should pray again for him. All those feelings of wanting to be the spiritual head of our house sprang up in my heart. My husband wasn't qualified to lead his family. I was. I prayed more than he did. I read my Bible more. I was more spiritual.

I even went so far as to think that I was more worthy of God than Steve was. How could he hear from the Lord if he didn't pray enough? How could he hear from the Lord if he didn't spend a lot of time in prayer? How could he know what direction our family was to go if he didn't spend enough time reading the "right" scriptures?

I reconciled myself to the fact that I would just have to be the spiritual leader in our home until Steve pulled himself into shape.

I decided that I must pray for Steve to become the godly man that I wanted and expected him to be.

The more I prayed for Steve, the less willing I was to relinquish spiritual headship to him. One day, he called to tell me he had witnessed to a young lady, and she had asked the Lord to enter her life. I am appalled now to think of my reaction. I thought, "He probably didn't do it right."

If one of the children asked a spiritual question at dinner, I was quick to jump in with an answer. I didn't want Steve to lead the prayers at home, because I felt he wasn't as "in touch" with the Lord as I was. Taking care of all the spiritual matters in our house had become second nature to me. I decided which church we would go to. I decided if our children went to Sunday School or not. I decided which passages of Scripture we would memorize. After all, I reasoned, if I didn't do it, who would?

5
If it Weren't for ME...

Apparently, my prayers for Steve weren't working. He wasn't changing. I began to grow disheartened. And so I decided I would look through the Bible, and find myself a real "man" I could have as my spiritual leader. I wanted to know what qualities he had, so I could pray more effectively for Steve.

As I began my search for the "perfect" spiritual leader, what I found astounded me. There was no one, except Jesus himself, who I would have followed. Each person I picked had something wrong with him, something that I could look at and say disqualified him from being the spiritual leader in my home.

For instance, I had always thought King David was a great guy. I mean, who wouldn't want a king for a husband? Yet, as I read about David's life, I realized that I would have problems with him as my spiritual leader. He committed adultery with Bathsheba. He had her husband sent off to battle and killed to cover his sin and the resulting pregnancy. And, as if that weren't bad enough, he turned a blind eye when his son raped his daughter, and then allowed another son to kill his brother. No, David did not seem to be the spiritual leader I was searching for.

It was about this time that the Lord revealed to me my own sin. I was reluctant at first to admit that I was sinning. Many sermons, friends, and books helped bring the point home. If I was doing everything to be the spiritual leader in our home, why did Steve need to do anything? I had been praying for Steve to get to the place where he could lead our family. At last, I realized he couldn't do that if I was always standing in his way.

After many tears of repentance, I finally realized that I was not the one who was supposed to take over the role of spiritual leader. Now that I had it figured out, what was I supposed to do? I had been doing all the spiritual leading in our house. How could I just walk away from that?

Again, I had to turn to the Lord to guide me.

I had one of those "yeah, but" prayer sessions with Him. I said, "Lord, you will need to help me slowly step out of this role." His response was that it must not be a slow process. I needed to do it *now*.

"Yeah, but, you don't understand, Lord. If I step out now, no one is going to pick up where I leave off."

The Lord kept pressing in, telling me that I was to step out. Now.

Finally, I stopped saying "yeah, but," and began to walk with the Lord.

This is when the Lord began to teach me about submission. This is when He revealed to me what the verse in Genesis is really talking about.

Have you ever wondered where Adam was while Eve was looking longingly at the forbidden fruit? He was right there with her. Why didn't he tell the serpent that he was lying, and to shut up? For that matter, why didn't he jump right in there and slay the serpent?

Adam was a wimp in the garden. He did nothing to stop Eve from sinning. He just stood there, and took the fruit willingly from Eve. Instead of remaining a perfect husband, he *allowed* Eve to rule over him.

And she, instead of remaining a perfect wife, took away her husband's authority. She decided to sin, and he allowed it. Ever since Eve, women have desired to be in charge. But God has given husbands that place of leadership.

Finally, I realized that I really was participating in the full curse, not just the childbearing part.

When I first heard about the concept of submitting to your spouse, I thought of submission in a purely physical way. I thought submitting meant that, if my husband wanted me sexually, then I was to say yes. Even though that was what I believed, I did not even practice that kind of submission. How sad that, through all those years of being married, I missed one of the greatest blessings the Lord has to offer.

The mere mention of the word submission caused me to flinch. All I thought it meant was that, for the rest of my life, I would no longer be me, Terri Sween Camp. Only Mrs. Steve Camp. I would lose my identity. I would be unable to function in society. Everything that made me what I was would disappear.

As the Lord began to show me my sinful heart with regard to submission, I began to explore what submission to my husband really meant. I first learned what submission did not mean. It did not mean that I was a lesser person. It did not mean that I was to roll over and let Steve walk all over me. It did not mean that, for the rest of my life, I was not to speak what was on my mind.

So what did it mean?

"Wives, submit to your own husbands, as to the Lord. For the husband is head of the wife, as also Christ is head of the church; and He is the Savior of the body. Therefore, just as the church is subject to Christ, so let the wives be to their own husbands in everything" (Ephesians 5:22-24).

Whoa! Does that really mean that I am to submit to my husband as to the Lord?

Why do we sometimes have problems with plain English? Yes. It means that I am to see my husband as head of me, just as Christ is head of the church. And Christ is the Savior of the body. So marriage is modeled after the church. Someone has to be the head. There isn't a lot that a body can accomplish without a head.

When I make a conscious effort to submit everything to my husband, I am in essence submitting my all to Jesus Christ. My willingness to accept all that my husband decides is like me telling Jesus, "I know you know what is best. You placed this husband at my head, and I will accept all that comes with that."

But, what about his part?

My husband is to love me as he loves Christ.

For the first time, I wondered, "Could his love be hindered by my lack of submission?"

I thought of an extreme example. If I am in control of our family and someone breaks into our house with a gun, threatening to kill everyone unless one person will sacrifice himself, and I am the one who has been "leading" the family, it might be pretty difficult for my husband to lay down his life willingly for me. He might be tempted to turn to me and say, "Hey, you've been the leader. You lay down your life."

But if I have had a submissive heart and attitude all along, my husband will know that he is the one who must lay down his life.

Now that the Lord had shown me the truth, I thought life would certainly be easy.

It was not. I still had to deal with my own "self" getting in the way. I was so used to making decisions in our home. I had to learn to step aside. Sometimes, the reminders that I was to step aside were right there in front of my face. Sometimes, I had to make some big mistakes to see how I was wrong. And sometimes, I had to confess my sin before I could move on.

I always hate confessing my sin to Steve. Confession may be good for the soul, but I have such a hard time. Somehow, I think that Steve can't possibly know that I sin. How ridiculous! He lives with me. How could he not see the sin in my life?

With the issue of submission, as hard as it was, I knew that my first order of business was to confess my sin to Steve. I needed him to hold me accountable for what the Lord had called me to do.

I went to Steve with a great deal of fear and trepidation. He didn't say much as I poured my heart out to him. As I told him that I had been taking a role that rightfully belonged to him, he stayed silent. I wondered if he had fallen asleep with his eyes open. I continued telling him what the Lord had told me to do. I even confessed to him that I originally went to the Lord to pray for him, but ended up being the one the Lord wanted to change. I finished up by telling him that he was to help me stay out of the spiritual leadership role.

He said, "Okay."

I felt better immediately. Then I began to wonder if I had really achieved the desired result. I mean, shouldn't Steve have said something that would indicate to me he was going to take an active interest in his role? Shouldn't he have said, "Let's pray"?

Oh, no! There I was, doing it all again. This stepping down was not going to be an easy thing.

At first, I had to be in constant prayer that the Lord would keep me out of the spiritual decision-making. After a while, I realized that I was not doing it anymore. The Lord had delivered me.

When I stepped aside, Steve stepped in.

It wasn't long before Steve was praying when he went to bed. One night, he couldn't sleep because a verse of Scripture kept coming into his head. Finally, he got up and opened his Bible. The verse given to him was in 1 Timothy 3. At the time, Steve had no clue what 1 Timothy 3 was about. As he began to read, he thought that the Lord was telling him that he was to be a pastor. He stayed up for hours with the Lord that night.

In the morning, Steve shared with me his night of being awake with the Lord. He read me this passage: "This is a faithful saying: If a man desires the position of a bishop, he desires a good work. A bishop then must be blameless, the husband of one wife, temperate, sober-minded, of good behavior, hospitable, able to teach; not given to wine, not violent, not greedy for money, but gentle, not quarrelsome, not covetous; one who rules his own house well, having his children in submission with all reverence (for if a man does not know how to rule his own house, how will he take care of the church of God?); not a novice, lest being puffed up with pride he fall into the same condemnation as the devil. Moreover he must have a good testimony among those who are outside, lest he fall into reproach and the snare of the devil" (1 Timothy 3:1-7).

When Steve told me that he felt he had been called by God to be a pastor, my first thought was, "God isn't calling you to be a pastor through those words. He is telling you that you have a long way to go."

Fortunately, I kept that to myself.

Of course, the Lord had to deal with me once again for my attitude. He had to remind me that I had stepped aside, and He was taking over.

This stepping aside took place many years ago. And a most amazing thing happened in our lives. Steve began to change. As I read the verse Steve was given, I thought that the only part that qualified him as a pastor was that he was the husband of one wife.

Now, when I look at the verse, I can use it as a measurement to see how far Steve has come since I stepped aside. But that isn't my job.

Just a few months ago, Steve and I were lying in bed talking and praying. Out of the blue, he said to me, "Do you know what has made the biggest impact in my life besides my salvation?" I didn't know, so he told me. "It was the day you came to me and told me that you had been taking my role as spiritual leader and you weren't going to do it anymore."

6
Bonk

You'd think that I could learn a lesson once and not have to repeat it over and over again.

Not me.

I long to have the Lord perfect me, but then, I mess up once more. I often wonder if the Lord looks down on me, and sighs, the way I sometimes sigh at the shenanigans of my toddler. We've told our children hundreds of times to put the tops back on the markers. But still I find markers all over the house with the tops left off. I would much rather throw out the markers than the children, but it is frustrating that they don't learn their lessons easily.

I am equally frustrated by my own inability to learn my lessons. Sometimes, I am sailing smoothly through life thinking, "Hey, I have this all together. I am a submissive wife." Then Steve tells me that something I have my heart set on doing has to be cancelled, and right away I know how far I am from having that all-together, submissive attitude.

Only recently, Steve called from work to tell me we wouldn't able to go on a trip I was really looking forward to. The forecast was for freezing rain.

My brain did not hear what he said. It interpreted his words as, "I don't want to go on this trip, and so I'm looking for any excuse to not go." I accused him, in my mind, of having a bad attitude.

I wonder what is wrong with me, when my own attitude stinks and I can't seem to change it. Instead of doing the right thing, as a submissive wife, I called the person we were going to visit and said, "Let's keep our options open, just in case it doesn't turn icy."

I kept my bad attitude all night. I went to bed grouchy, and even snapped at Steve when he reminded me of the weather forecast. I said, "You don't really want to go." I reasoned that I was not being unsubmissive—except perhaps for the snappy comment. I was merely being more optimistic than Steve.

But that was not the attitude of my heart. Deep inside, I wanted to *prove* him wrong. The weather would be fine. We would be able to go, and we were going to have a great time.

Now I was guilty of the sin of pride, too.

I got up early to check the roads. They were still icy, but the temperature was warming up. I decided that we would be able to go. We would just have to leave a bit later.

I went back to our bedroom and informed Steve of *my* decision before climbing into bed for another hour.

Do you think I was able to sleep? No. Was I lying there repenting of my bad attitude? Of my pride? I was not. I was growing steadily angrier with Steve, for being so unsupportive. I lay in bed going over all the times I could remember when I thought Steve's attitude was bad. I even entertained thoughts like, "If I weren't married to him, I wouldn't have to put up with this garbage."

I don't know why God didn't immediately speak to my heart and convict me of my terrible attitude. But no. He let me go on and on, wallowing in my pride and sin.

Sometimes, I wish that He would, supernaturally speaking, bonk me on the head.

After entertaining those horrendous thoughts for a good forty-five minutes, I decided again to poke my head out of the door, to see the now-perfect road conditions. At that moment, the telephone rang. Steve answered, and told me that a friend, who knew we were planning the trip, had called cautioning us to stay home.

I was even more furious. I thought I detected an air of enjoyment in Steve's voice as he relayed the information. I stormed out of our room.

The Lord's "bonking" came as I was descending the stairs. *Terri, you have a bad attitude.*

"No, I don't," I argued with my conscience.

Yes, you do.

By the time I reached the front door, I had already decided we weren't going. Not because the roads were bad, but because I knew that Steve's decision had been right all along. He did not want to risk the lives of his wife and children.

I could have stopped there and felt confident with my decision. But still I opened the door and went out to check the weather. It would have served me right to slip on the ice and break my back. But I didn't. I'm glad I don't always get what I deserve.

A few minutes later, Steve came down the stairs. "What are you doing up?" I asked.

He didn't know my heart had changed. He said, "I figured you were going with or without me. So you may as well go with me."

I smiled as I shook my head. "I'm sorry I had a bad attitude."

"You're forgiven," he said.

Hey! Wait a minute. He's supposed to say he's sorry too!

Then he said, "I'm sorry too."

I wonder which one of us the Lord is trying to perfect. Could it be we needed a dual "bonking"?

"Not that I have already attained, or am already perfected; but I press on, that I may lay hold of that for which Christ Jesus has also laid hold of me" (Philippians 3:12).

PART TWO:
COMMUNICATING IN BABEL

7
Almost Perfect

I remember once telling Steve, before we were married, that I thought he was perfect. He quickly put me in my place, reminding me that no one is perfect. To which I, in the greatest form of argument I could muster to win, replied, "I meant you are perfect for me." Still stumbling over my words, never wanting to lose a verbal argument, I continued, "What I mean is, together, we make a perfect pair." There. I won.

To which he simply responded again, "No one is perfect." Okay, he won. But I wanted the romantic "aren't we perfect" scene, and he wanted the reality scene. I wasn't so sure a realist was exactly what I wanted. After all, I'm an idealist. Idealists and romanticists go together, not idealists and realists. Or so I thought.

Well, I married him anyway. I did, indeed, discover he was not perfect.

On the other hand, he never expected perfection from me, but he didn't realize how far short of it I would fall.

For instance, I really don't like to do dishes on a meal-by-meal basis. It's one of those crisis management jobs for me. When we have no more clean dishes, when all the paper plates are gone, and we are not going out to buy any more, either paper or china, then I figure it is time to wash the dishes.

Steve eventually came to accept my lack of training in the housekeeping department, and I began to have a ten-minute pickup time before he got home, being especially watchful for the stray Lego that was certain to show up under his foot as soon as he took off his shoes.

He even was able to accept my idealistic tendencies. And I soon realized that a realist and an idealist do make for very good mates. As much as it bugged me when he said that paying sixteen hundred dollars a month for the five-bedroom house I wanted was out of our budget.

"But it's such a lovely house," I pleaded. It was a long while before I began to see that God would use Steve to protect our family and our marriage as long as I was his helpmeet, and not his help-make-him-change-his-mind-meet.

Just the other day, however, he did say to me, "You know, you'd be perfect if it wasn't for that one fault." I hesitantly asked him what that one fault was. You'll never guess what he said.

First, notice that he has gone from saying "nobody's perfect" to saying I'm about as close as they come. In his book, anyway. So I may not have won the argument way back then, but after sixteen years of marriage, he has almost changed his mind. Which is good, because I have this problem. Not a fault that would keep me from being a perfect wife, but a simple problem. I like to be right. And I like to *prove* I am right. I want everyone to *admit* that I am right. I suppose it has something to do with growing up with a lawyer for a father.

And I was right. We are "perfect." For each other.

Oh. Except for that one fault Steve just mentioned that keeps me from being a perfect wife.

I don't make spaghetti often enough for dinner.

Shamefacedly, I have to admit to it. Now, if I could only fix that problem, I would be perfect.

8
The Way to a Man's Heart

Everyone has heard the cliché: "The way to a man's heart is through his stomach." Well, in Steve's case, that is sometimes true. So why don't I fix my one fault, and make him spaghetti as often as he would like it?

For one thing, I'm not a big food person. Being in the kitchen isn't my idea of the way to spend an afternoon. I prefer to whip up food the moment we need it.

This, of course, doesn't usually work, because I tend to get busy with what I am doing throughout the day, and forget that everyone else in the house is famished. So, over the years, I have had to develop a kitchen plan of action.

When I had just a couple of little children, they subsisted on cereal, cold wieners, macaroni and cheese, and an occasional vegetable.

Vegetables were the first food-related problem Steve and I had, apart from the fact that I thought he could perhaps bring dinner home every night. Every few weeks, Steve would casually mention that we hadn't eaten any vegetables at all.

I do not like vegetables. Green vegetables are the worst. And I'm not terribly fond of the orange ones either. Yellow vegetables are all right, but I have found out they don't really count, nutritionally, as vegetables. I was certain, however, that potato chips counted as a vegetable, and we had plenty of those.

Finally, Steve convinced me that I was to serve vegetables with almost every meal. Bleck! But I began to stomach making vegetables each night. That doesn't mean I ate them, but I did prepare them.

Our children learned to love veggies. I had to begin telling them, "You may not have more spinach until you eat that hot dog."

Once, when we had three little ones, my dad and his wife took us to a great restaurant at Fisherman's Wharf in San Francisco. They were amazed that my girls ate all the broccoli on their plates, and even wanted my vegetables too. Which I generously gave them. We then ventured over to the Ghirardelli Chocolate Factory. One bite of chocolate, and our dear Christi made a dreadful face. "I don't like that!" She has since been cured of her chocolate loathing.

I could not take any credit for my broccoli-loving children, but eventually began to eat broccoli itself, even though it was green. I even began to enjoy it. But I still did not want to spend a great deal of time in the kitchen. What was the point in taking all that time to prepare a meal? It was devoured in ten minutes, and then I had to spend another forty minutes cleaning up the mess.

Also, I had a number of flops in the kitchen, before and shortly after I was married. I remember my first attempt at mashed potatoes. Someone told me you had to cook them for an hour. So I dropped them into a pan of boiling water, and went to a friend's house. When I returned, the potatoes were charred. And the pan was ruined. So much for impressing my dad with my culinary skills. I hadn't planned anything else to eat with the mashed potatoes, so we went out for pizza.

My sister always joked that I would never be a good cook. Perhaps it is my inability to focus on one task at a time. I always seem to forget something fairly important to the recipe, like eggs, or flour. I could never make a decent chocolate chip cookie. The first time Steve asked me to make them, I was mortified. Didn't he know I was cookie challenged? Did I fail to mention that before the wedding? Why didn't he tell me how much he liked fresh chocolate chip cookies every week?

Finally, after many attempts, I was able to make a decent chocolate chip cookie.

But then came the request for spaghetti. Spaghetti sauce is probably my least favorite thing to make. I'm sure it all stems from the time I was following a recipe and accidentally put three tablespoons of brown sugar into the sauce instead of one teaspoon. I think I started reading the recipe on the opposite page.

The other thing I did regularly was burn the sauce. Spaghetti sauce requires that you actually stir it frequently while it is cooking. Who has time to stir?

I once read that you could place marbles in the bottom of the pan and that, as the pan heated, it would cause the marbles to run around the bottom of the pan, acting like a stirrer. It didn't work. I ended up wasting an entire month's worth of spaghetti sauce.

Making spaghetti also causes a horrible mess. It requires at least three pans: one to brown the ground beef, one to cook the sauce, and one to cook the noodles. And then you need a strainer to drain the noodles. That is way too many dishes for one meal. Then, to top it off, the stove always gets disgusting spots of sauce all over the top. And if these are left to sit for weeks, they can be really difficult to clean off.

So, that is why I don't make spaghetti as often as Steve would like.

But I have learned to make some awesome whole-wheat bread with freshly ground flour. Now there is a kitchen duty I can enjoy. It's actually more like therapy. I first had the idea of making my own bread when a pregnant friend, who had five children already, brought us a meal when we moved into our new house. She brought spaghetti (can you believe it?), lettuce salad, and fresh homemade bread. I thought to myself, "If this woman can do it, I can too."

So I began making bread. Steve kindly bought me a KitchenAid mixer to make my life easier. But then I discovered the Bosch. I was certain he would not get me a Bosch after he just bought me a KitchenAid. When I presented the idea to him at the table one night, I expected I would have to do the quiet submissive sulk. Instead, he heard me out, and simply said, "Okay, you may get it."

Thus began the bread-making business, which our oldest daughter has now taken over to pay for her horses.

I would like to mention that the friend who brought over the fresh bread that day later confessed to me that she did not actually make the bread herself. It was a frozen loaf that she simply thawed and put in the oven.

It made me wonder, why do we do things just because other people do them? One of my mom's favorite sayings when I was a child was, "If they jumped off a bridge, would you do that too?"

Why do we look at other Christians and see the outward things they do, and desire to do those things?

9
The Search for the Perfect Wife

Have you ever gone through the Bible looking for the "perfect wife"? Surely, somewhere in Scripture there is the one person God wants us to be like. One woman who encompasses all those traits of biblical character that we could simply read about and copy? Better yet, wouldn't it be great if someone like that moved in next door? We could put a web cam in her living room and view firsthand what the perfect wife does and does not do.

Don't we all look at other women in our church and want to be them? We see them from afar and think, "If only I could be like her, then I would be the "perfect wife."

My first experience with wanting to emulate one of those women came when I met a dear sweet lady at the church where I was saved. She had five children, and homeschooled them all. I had only two children at the time, and I couldn't believe it. Watching her had an enormous impact on my life. She was everything I wanted to be. I still cannot think of anything that she did that I did not want to do or become. She was the first woman who talked of children being obedient. She was the first woman I met who seemed genuinely to revere her husband. She was the first person I met who showed a genuine Christian love. I thought she was perfect. Actually, I still think she was perfect. I still want to be just like her.

Then I wanted to be like the pastor's wife. She, too, homeschooled her children. She was beautiful. Her husband adored her. Her house was always spotless. She did all kinds of crafts, so I wanted to do crafts too. I bought a glue gun, and everyone on my Christmas list that year got a stupid homemade craft.

Several years later, we had the privilege of entertaining this dear woman and her husband with, would you believe, messed-up chocolate chip cookies. The cookies, at least that day, weren't my fault. Steve made them. Her husband loved them anyway.

As I was showing her around our house, she said to me, "I don't know how you do it."

I looked her in the eye and said, "You don't know how I do it? I don't know how *you* do it!" We both laughed, as we realized at the same time that we were looking at the externals of our lives, and thinking that we were falling apart, while everyone else had it all together. Meanwhile, people look at us and think we have it all together.

Women look at many externals. One of them is number of children. I'm delighted to say that I usually get a high score in the score-the-friend game. I do find it interesting, though, that a mom of eight will say *wow* when introduced to a mom of ten. A mom of ten will say *wow* when introduced to a mom of thirteen. A mom of thirteen will say, "I'm tired. And I don't have the patience of Job. I've just been blessed with a lot of children."

But we continue to look at the externals. If we walk into another woman's house that is perfectly clean, we go home and yell at our kids to clean up their messes. If there is a woman who does wonderful work with her hands, we go out and buy knitting needles or a glue gun. If there is a woman who wears a size six, we look in the mirror and say, "I'm fat."

This isn't a new generation of looking at the externals. I think that women have done this for centuries.

Think about Sarah and Hagar. Sarah and her husband Abram (Abraham) desperately wanted children. God had promised they would have offspring. But Sarah remained childless. In that culture, a stigma was attached to a woman without children. It was considered a curse, a judgment of God. So Sarah had good reasons for wanting children. Peer pressure was a motivation. So what did Sarah do? She encouraged her husband to bed Hagar, her personal servant, in order to have a child.

This is going just a bit too far in the quest to be the winner of the "perfect wife" game. You do not win by encouraging your husband to get another woman pregnant.

Even though Sarah's request sounds horrible to me, and even though she was lacking faith in God, I kind of understand where she was coming from. This woman wanted to please her husband.

When I read in Scripture that "Abram heeded the voice of Sarah" (Gen. 16:2), I sometimes shake my head in bewilderment. Hasn't this man read his Bible? Doesn't he know that the *man* is the head of the family? Doesn't he know what is bound to happen when he messes with another woman?

It's sometimes hard to understand these husbands of ours.

Have you ever wondered if the Tower of Babel confused the language between the sexes too?

10
No Hablo es Husbandese

"Come, let Us go down and there confuse their language, that they may not understand one another's speech" (Genesis 11:7).

I really do wonder if the language between men and women was also confused at this time. I must admit my husband and I do not always seem to speak the same language.

I learned my language as a young child from my mom. By observing her for many years, I learned a certain mode of behavior, which I have shared with my husband on many occasions. You see, my mom was a non-confrontational type. I thought that was good, since I too was a non-confrontational type. However, I often found my mom upset, or even in tears, because everything was not going according to her plan.

It's not that she was selfish. The problem was that she failed to verbalize her plans to everyone else in the family. Somehow, we were simply supposed to *know* what she had planned.

Well, I took up this attribute as I grew. Now, keeping thoughts to yourself is fine if you are single. However, if you are married, and you have certain expectations, it is often helpful to share them with the other people involved.

I remember when I planned to attend a family gathering at my dad's house with Steve and the kids. This meant we had to leave fairly early in the morning. The only plan I shared with Steve was that we needed to leave by ten o'clock. I failed to tell him that we had to bathe all the children, carry a couple of baskets of bread, stop at the car wash, and actually be on our way at ten o'clock.

Steve's plan was to get up at quarter to ten. He could easily be ready to go in fifteen minutes.

As I was running around frantically trying to get everyone and everything ready, he slept on. The longer he slept, the angrier I became. Every little thing that went wrong suddenly became his fault. He knew my plan. Why was he still sleeping?

Finally, he emerged from the bedroom, came downstairs, and said, "Why aren't you ready yet?"

I wanted to scream. So I did. "What do you mean, why aren't I ready yet? I've been running around like a madwoman, trying to get these kids all ready and get the food packed, and all you did to was *sleep*!" I ranted and raved. I'll spare you the details, for the sake of my dignity. Suffice it to say I was not the paragon of a loving wife. In fact, I was ready to call the whole thing off. I couldn't believe I was married to someone who didn't know, without being told, all that had to be done to prepare for our day out.

Fortunately, Steve was ever so kind, and only ignored me. If he had retaliated with harmful words, I don't know what I would have done.

I wish I could say that, as soon as I got in the van, the realization hit me that I was expecting him to read my mind. But it didn't. It took me several months, perhaps years, to figure out that Steve did not know how to read my mind.

So, I set out to help him. One day I was making dinner. The kids were running around the kitchen, and Steve was sitting in his chair. Having figured out that telling someone exactly what you expect is the best policy, I looked him square in the eye and said, "Now would be a good time for you to read my mind."

He looked at me and said, "What?"

What? What? How could he ask me that? He knew perfectly well what I was thinking. I wanted him to take the children out of the kitchen. I wanted him to take them out of the house. I needed some peace and quiet. How could he not just *know* that? His innocent look did not fool me. He knew exactly what I was thinking and was refusing to meet my needs. Or so I thought. (Good thing he couldn't read that one.)

Then it dawned on me. He cannot read my mind. He does not have a clue that the children are irritating me. If I want him to meet my needs, then I have to make those needs known to him. Then, if he doesn't do what I want, I can be mad at him. But I need to give him a chance.

So I said, "Do you think you could take the kids outside and play with them?"

"Sure," he said. "Great idea."

I walked away, perplexed. How could I have let so many years go past, with all that misunderstanding, when all I had to do was speak, rather than thinking he should know what I was thinking?

I'm happy to report that I have mastered the concept of telling Steve what is on my mind, rather than expecting him to know. But I do occasionally relapse and announce to him, "Now would be a good time to read my mind."

And he almost always says, "What?"

It can be frustrating. But it is also comforting.

There are some secrets I would like to keep.

11
Matters of the Heart

A few times in my married life, I have been glad Steve couldn't read my mind.

There was a time, not terribly long ago, when I was confronted with a problem that I was unable to conquer on my own. It was a sin of my heart.

Often I have asked God why He gives me choices in life. I would much rather be told what to do and when to do it, and have absolutely no choice in the matter. This, to me, would be a perfect world.

Sadly, we live in a fallen world. I would prefer to be a perfect sinless being, but I am not capable of that. Even though I desire to walk upright and blameless as a child of God, I cannot. I am a sinner, and it drives me crazy.

When I became saved, I begged God to give me a list of rules and regulations. I took out my Bible and began reading it from cover to cover, highlighting all the text that gave me a direction, either to follow or not. My Bible was covered in orange highlighter. There seemed to be so many things that we are to do or not do. I began to feel overwhelmed. And I had only gotten to Leviticus.

I asked a godly woman I knew how she was able to live a pure and holy life. I then asked her about a few of the commands in the Old Testament. She told me, "I have enough trouble following the New Testament to worry about following all the rules of the Law in the Old Testament."

My cover-to-cover Bible search skipped a few books. I began underlining in the New Testament. The more of God's commands I underlined, the worse I felt. Then, I had a shining moment. I discovered grace, and learned of repentance. I felt better knowing that, if I repent of my sins, I am walking in perfection because the shed blood of Jesus covers all my wrongdoing.

Then, something horrible happened to me. I was filled in my heart with unclean thoughts for another man. I looked at him as a spiritual giant in his family. He knew the Bible well. He led his family in devotions. He desired to live his life for Jesus. I was attracted to his zeal for the Lord. I was attracted to his love for his family and his desire to spend time with his children. For days, I spent every waking moment thinking of this man.

I was consumed. I cried out to God to take away these thoughts, and in the morning I woke up to find them once again taking over. I began to feel dejected and defeated. So I went to His Word.

I read, in Matthew's gospel: "You have heard that it was said to those of old, 'You shall not commit adultery.' But I say to you that whoever looks at a woman to lust for her has already committed adultery with her in his heart" (Matt. 5:27-30).

God led me to this passage. I assumed, based on the thoughts going on in my heart, that it doesn't speak only to men. I knew that I must take captive the thoughts of my heart. But how?

I could not stop seeing this man. He was a part of our lives. Our family spent time with his family on a regular basis. What was I to do? I felt immobilized by my thoughts. That passage about adultery is followed by a verse that says if our eye causes us to sin, we are to pluck it out. If our hand causes us to sin, we are to cut it off. I wondered how, exactly, I was going to pluck out my heart.

Steve had noticed that I was troubled. How could I act normally? My thoughts were unclean. He asked me what was wrong. Of course, there was no way I was going to tell him! But then I felt a prompting from God that I must confess my unclean thoughts to my husband.

"No way!" I thought. "I'm not going to do that. It will hurt him. He will hate me. He will want a divorce." All of those thoughts came to my mind as I heard my lips say, "I need to talk to you."

I followed him to our bedroom. As he changed from his work clothes, I began pouring out my heart to him. With tears in my eyes, I told him how sorry I was for the thoughts I had been thinking. He took me in his arms and confessed to me that he too, had unclean thoughts that he had to take captive. He held me for a long time that afternoon. Together we healed what had become a wound in our relationship. Together we prayed to God to help us keep the thoughts that are unclean out of our hearts. That afternoon, I learned many great truths in my life. I learned that my husband loved me unconditionally. I learned that, even though I might have unclean thoughts from time to time, God does take them from me if I am faithful to repent.

I did not tell Steve who the unclean thoughts were about. I valued the friendship we had with the family of this man and felt that, if I were to reveal his identity to Steve, he would not want to sit under his teaching again. But, the next time we gathered together with that family, I felt nothing but a genuine Christ-like love for the man. My thoughts were held captive.

Unfortunately, I still have to deal with unclean thoughts in my heart. Even while I long to be perfect, sometimes I even *allow* such thoughts to remain with me. Not long ago, I sat in church while our pastor was giving a lovely sermon, enjoying my unclean thoughts, and not even repentant.

We always sit in the second pew at our church. No one sits in the front pew. In other words, we are right there under the eye of the pastor. I have sometimes accused him of thinking about particular members of his congregation when he gives his sermons. Of course, as he stares out across the pews, who sticks out like a sore thumb? Me! Yes, I often believe that he writes his sermons just for me. Everyone else gets to listen to the pastor preaching to me.

That's the way it was on this particular day. I was sitting there, enjoying my unclean thoughts, when the pastor began talking about temptations. He caught my attention. He went on to talk about enjoying our temptations. The rest of the congregation might as well have gone out for coffee. He was talking to me. I know he was even staring right at me, though he claimed he wasn't. He talked about how we allow Satan to get just a little foot inside the door of our lives. In my heart I knew that I wasn't only letting his foot in. I saw myself flinging the door wide open. The more the pastor talked, the more I felt that I must once again take those thoughts captive. I saw myself taking the knob of the door that I had flung open. I slammed it shut. And the thoughts I had been enjoying were gone.

I suddenly found that I had surrendered my thoughts to the Lord. It's only when we surrender everything to God that we can walk fully with Him.

PART THREE:
MAGNIFYING MOMENTS

12
Letting God Be in Control

I am convinced in my heart that many of the struggles we have in this life, many of our concerns, really boil down to one simple factor. When we receive Christ into our hearts, we ask Him to be Lord of our lives. What does that mean? It means that we are no longer our own person, but that we are His. We are His to do with us whatever He pleases.

We may be fine with that in many areas of our lives. But there are some areas we simply don't want to surrender to Him. This is an ongoing struggle. However, I have yet to learn of a struggle that my God cannot overcome.

Many of the struggles in our lives we cannot control. Those are easy to give over to God. If we cannot control them, then we pass them off. However, with the issue of letting God plan our families, there is the ability to control it. So, we want to do that.

Many people counseled us, following the birth of our second daughter, and my postpartum hemorrhage, that two children was enough. We were not Christians at the time, but are very thankful that we did not heed this advice. It was then that our children began coming by Cesarean section. First came Cathy, at three weeks late, then David, also three weeks late. Next came John, a neatly scheduled C-section. We had not been convinced that God was in control. We were still in control, even though we were allowing the children to come as they may.

I remember so well the trip home from the hospital after I had John. I cried as Steve told me he had decided we would have no more children. But really, I felt fine about the decision. After all, I could see all the reasons for not having more children. There was the question of money, of course. But Steve's biggest concern was for my well-being.

I won't kid you. It was tough having five children all under seven years old. The house was never in order, I often felt overwhelmed, and I could never seem to get myself all together. But all this meant that I had to cling constantly to my Savior. How my faith grew in those years.

The decision had been made however, and there would be no more little Campers. Fortunately for me, my husband did nothing practical to act on that decision, and I became pregnant with our daughter Briana. She was our sixth in nine years. Throughout my entire pregnancy with her, Steve told me she would *definitely* be our last.

I knew that I must surrender this issue to God. Steve did not have the same conviction. He still wanted to be in control. The story of Briana's birth is too long to retell here.* However, we believe God gave us a miracle by allowing her to be born without a C-section. It was through much prayer that she came into this world. Through her, my faith increased. I grew closer to the Lord.

Steve was still not convinced that God knew what He was doing. Oh, he wouldn't have said it that way. But that was how he felt at the time. He even claims that he had a bargain with God. Steve would allow God to do whatever He saw fit as far as our family size. At the same time, he felt as though God had told him that He wouldn't allow any more children to be born into our home.

It was a bit unsettling to me when I found out I was pregnant with our seventh child. Yes, I was overjoyed, but the prospect of telling Steve dampened my joy. Finally, I simply had to tell him. He was not happy. He felt betrayed by God. It took three days for God to get hold of Steve's heart. If we had taken things into our own hands, the following blessing would not have happened to us. God turned Steve from looking at children as just an extension of him, and turned Steve into a father who valued his children more than life itself. I cannot even begin to explain the blessing that this was to our family. What if we had stopped after two children?

We began a process of surrendering everything to God. Our faith in Christ as a family grew by leaps and bounds because of this surrender.

One morning in June, I went to the doctor because I thought I had a bladder infection. On the way there I realized that I could be pregnant. I hadn't even thought about the possibility before then.

Sure enough, I had both a bladder infection, and a growing baby. This time, Steve met the news of my pregnancy with a shout of "hallelujah!" How the Lord had changed his heart! We rejoiced together, knowing that God created our unborn child just for us. And that, through yet another child, our faith would grow.

13
I Will Bless the Lord

"I will bless the LORD at all times; His praise shall continually be in my mouth. My soul shall make its boast in the LORD; The humble shall hear of it and be glad. Oh, magnify the LORD with me, And let us exalt His name together" (Psalm 34:1-3).

Have you ever had one of those "magnifying" moments in your life? A little over three years ago I had a "magnifying" moment. The impending birth of my child was supposed to be just an ordinary moment. I know that each birth is a precious moment and that every child is a gift from God. Yet, after having given birth to seven children already, the event was supposed to be reasonably ordinary and uneventful.

However, the birth of Bryan was anything but ordinary.

The memory is still so vivid that the mere thought of it brings tears to my eyes. I can watch the moment unfold in my mind's eye. I can still feel the dread that overcame me as I first saw the toilet that I had filled with blood. I can still hear the tremble in my husband's voice as he called our family to pray. The look of the ambulance crewmember's face when he walked into the bathroom that was soaked with blood is still sharp in my mind. I can feel the bitter cold that penetrated every part of my being. The teeth chattering that would not stop. The unquenchable need for warmth that could not be achieved.

Time stands still as I remember hearing that my unborn child still had a heartbeat, even though it was faint. The only thought that gripped me as I lay on the hospital bed was that I might lose my baby.

I can still sense the calm that engulfed me as I waited for the birth. I felt certain that I was going to die. But I felt no fear. I felt the Lord holding me in His arms as I drifted between sleep and wakefulness. The glow in the operating room reminded me of heaven. As I was put to sleep, I was certain I would wake up in Glory with my newborn child.

However, I awakened in a new glory. The glory of knowing that there is a plan and purpose for every one of us. And that we don't know where the path may lead. I was often trying to peek around the corners to see where the Lord was taking me. In the past three years, He has taught me simply to walk with Him.

I often refer to this as a "magnifying" moment, one that changed the course of my life. Not that I suddenly became someone different. I did not. What I mean is that I experienced a sudden, obvious, hit-me-over-the-head kind of knowledge of how big this world is, yet how much bigger is the God that I serve.

I saw a God who performed a miracle in allowing me to live, though I needed twelve units of blood.

I saw a God who multiplied the blessing of the birth of our son Bryan. He is not just a son to us. He is a testimony of the miraculous healing power of our Lord. He is living proof that God is in control of every situation. He reminds us what a blessing it is to desire children, and to allow God to plan the size of our family.

If we had decided to stop having children, and actually prevented their conception, we would have missed out on the blessing of the incredible miracles that we saw with Bryan. Again, our faith increased.

Letting God plan your family size is not only about the children. It is also about what happens in your spiritual walk when you are willing to surrender even your very lives to the will of the Father.

Bigger even than that was the discovery that God could take such a moment in *my* life, and use it to reach hundreds, even thousands of people.

It's not that He thought anything great about me, or that I was some super, nearly sinless Christian. I can assure you that I was not. I'm still not there. Yet God still chose to use me. I often shake my head in disbelief. Doesn't He know that I forget to do the dishes? Doesn't He know that I have sin in my life? Doesn't He know that I haven't dusted my mini-blinds? Doesn't He know that almost every time I sit down to read my Bible, something, or someone interrupts me? Really, I'm a nobody, not worthy of receiving a blessing from Him. Certainly not the blessing of being a spokesman for Him.

But then, as I read the Bible, I'm often confronted with other "nobodies" that God has used. Scripture is filled with the stories of "nobodies."

I wonder if any of them sat around with their friends saying, "Why did God pick me?" Do you think Paul ever questioned why he was chosen? He's the last person I would have considered. Or how about Jonah? Jonah didn't even want to obey God. But God still chose him to go to Nineveh and preach about His mercy and love. God is always choosing people who aren't perfect. Why is that?

"For this reason I bow my knees to the Father of our Lord Jesus Christ, from whom the whole family in heaven and earth is named, that He would grant you, according to the riches of His glory, to be strengthened with might through His Spirit in the inner man, that Christ may dwell in your hearts through faith; that you, being rooted and grounded in love, may be able to comprehend with all the saints what is the width and length and depth and height—to know the love of Christ which passes knowledge; that you may be filled with all the fullness of God" (Ephesians 3:14-19).

That's why God chose Paul, and Jonah, and you and me. Not for His sake, but for ours: so that we may know the width and length and depth and height of His love.

"Now to Him who is able to do exceedingly abundantly above all that we ask or think, according to the power that works in us, to Him be glory in the church by Christ Jesus to all generations, forever and ever. Amen" (Ephesians 3:20,21).

14
It's Over!

One day, at a midweek prayer meeting in the midst of my seemingly content life, I realized there was so much of the Lord that I was missing. I felt far from Him, and I wondered how I could achieve that closeness with Him that I so desired.

Rarely in my life have I been satisfied with the status quo. If I am not moving forward, I feel that I am moving backward. Moving away from the Lord is a terrifying thought to me. I never want to be in a place where I feel I am not moving forward with Him.

I had heard a sermon about how God uses trials to draw us closer to Him. And so I prayed that the Lord would bring me a trial that would force me to turn to Him. I have since decided I am *never* going to pray such a prayer again. There have been other times in my life when I prayed and had to wait for the answer. But God chose to answer this one right away.

The trials came quickly. They were little things at first, but they began to mount up. I'm not even sure that the trials ever really increased in scope; it was just that they became stacked one upon another.

I had just begun to homeschool my oldest. I had four children under six years old. My days were filled with messes, and diapers, of tending to everyone but me. The last thing I wanted at the end of the day was to have my husband come home and demand more of me. I began to look at the demands I felt he was placing on me, everything from breakfast to bed, as irritations in my life.

I was ready to get out. This marriage and family thing was not what I expected it to be. I did not feel I was equipped to handle it all.

The more I rebelled, the more it seemed Steve demanded from me. Imagine, he actually wanted to eat off real dishes. And clean ones, at that! He wanted a home that was not disgusting to live in. But it was. It seemed that, the more I tried to do, the further behind I got. I was pulled in so many directions that I was cracking under the pressure.

I began seriously to think about going through divorce proceedings. Somehow, I thought that Steve was the problem. I prayed for him all the time. I went through the house singing, as loud as I could, the song *My House* by Ron David Moore. The song takes the words from the Bible: "My house will be a house of purity. My house will be a house of prayer." As I sang, I thought of all the things Steve was doing that I looked at as sin against God. In other words, I used this song to express my anger toward Steve. I sang it over and over again. I would begin to feel puffed up. I was the righteous one and Steve was the one who was always sinning.

It is a long hard painful fall from the top of the ladder of self-righteousness.

Early in the day, I had changed yet another diaper. On my way to the garbage bin, the phone rang. I put the dirty diaper down on the dishwasher as I picked up the phone. After hanging up the phone, one of the children demanded my attention. I forgot all about the diaper. This is characteristic of me. I tend to be flighty when it comes to domestic things.

When Steve arrived home that evening, I told him he needed to return a call. Walking to the phone, he spied the dirty diaper, still sitting on the dishwasher. I'm sure for him it was the last straw in an already disgusting house.

At the same time, I was complaining to him from across the room. He picked up the diaper and flung it as hard as he could toward me. He wasn't trying to hit me. He just wanted to throw it in my general direction. Well, instead of hitting me, he hit our wedding picture, hanging on the wall.

As I saw the diaper make impact and shatter the glass, I took it as a sign that indeed our marriage was over. There was no salvaging it at that point. The pieces had shattered, and there was no putting it back together. All that was left was to throw it into the garbage.

For several months, I was certain there wasn't anything left of our marriage. Oh, I still told Steve that I loved him, and tried to pretend that I felt something, but I felt nothing. I had stopped sobbing long ago. Now, sweeping up the shattered glass from our wedding picture, the tears came again.

I don't know how I continued to function. My every waking moment was consumed with thoughts of divorce. Steve's sins played repeatedly in my mind. Every time I closed my eyes, I saw the diaper sail past me, shattering the picture.

Steve no longer attended church with me much, so I asked if I could go to a different church. That was fine with him. The next Sunday, I packed the four little children into the car and headed off to a new church. I wore my grubbiest jeans, because I wanted to see if the people in the church judged others by the way they dressed. As soon as I walked in the door I knew that the Lord was there. I was immediately welcomed, grubby jeans and all.

I don't remember the sermon that day, but I do remember that we sang, over and over again, a song called *When My Heart is Overwhelmed*. As I sang the words, about the Lord leading me to the Rock when my heart is overwhelmed, I suddenly was flooded with thoughts of my own sin. I cried and cried. As we continued to sing, my heart was broken. But at the same time, in just a matter of minutes, the Lord came and ministered to me. I realized that the only way I was going to make it through life was if I clung to the Lord. There was no other way. I could not do it on my own. I could not get through life by getting divorced from my husband. Divorce was suddenly not an option. Even if my life was crummy, my Lord could give me the joy I so craved.

I left the church that morning a different person from the one who had walked in the door.

Almost immediately upon arriving home, Steve looked at me and asked, "What happened? You're glowing."

I told him, "I sat at the feet of Jesus today."

The next week, Steve was anxious to go to this church that changes people. He too found himself in the presence of Jesus. As the people there embraced us with their love, and as we embraced Jesus, Steve and I found ourselves once again embracing each other. Our lives began to be transformed. The year of trial had come to a close.

When we were in the midst of that stormy time, I saw no end. But now, at the end, I saw the fruition of my prayer to draw closer to my Lord. I still wouldn't recommend praying for trials! I have learned, though, that the best way to get through whatever the Lord sends me is to cling to Him with all my might.

We bought a new piece of glass for our wedding picture, but it still sits on top of the kitchen cabinets. I don't have the heart to replace it. You see, every time I look at that picture of Steve and me on the day we said, "Until death do us part," it is a constant reminder that a marriage that is not rooted in the Lord can so easily be shattered by our own sinful thoughts and self-righteousness.

I must always look to Jesus to clean me up. I cannot look at Steve and demand that the Lord clean him, but only that He clean me. I pray for Steve, but it is so easy to dwell on his sins, when my own list is at least as long. I must get my focus off of the person I cannot change, and on to the person I can. I need to ask the Lord to change me.

15
Seek Him

I love the translation of Jeremiah 29:11-13 in the Amplified Bible: "For I know the thoughts *and* plans that I have for you, says the Lord, thoughts *and* plans for welfare *and* peace, and not for evil, to give you hope in your final outcome. Then you will call upon Me, and you will come and pray to Me, and I will hear *and* heed you. Then you will seek Me, inquire for *and* require Me [as a vital necessity] and find Me; when you search for Me with all your heart."

I often wish I could always be in that place of continually walking with God, of always longing for His presence, of always seeking Him. But I'm not. Sometimes, it takes particular events in my life to bring me back to the place where I am always supposed to be.

I've often heard people say, "Well, there's nothing left but prayer." It is as though prayer is a way of giving up. But that's not how it should be for the Christian. The Christian should have the attitude, "I will pray and God will hear my prayer."

We all know that is the attitude we should have. But we don't always have it.

Sometimes, we want to share our misery with all of our friends before we are willing to commit it to God. I've even heard some women say that they don't go to Mom's Night Out meetings or ladies' Bible studies because the women tend to bring before the group all their woes with their husbands. "My husband never plays with the kids." Or, "I can't get my husband to do anything around the house." And I'm sure you've all heard, "I would get rid of the television if it weren't for my husband being addicted to it."

These attitudes sadden me. They sadden me because I can see myself reflected in these statements. It reminds me that I used to call up my friends and gripe about my husband. Or I would call my mom and tell her how mean he was, or how unfairly he was treating me.

It was when I was encouraged by another woman to let my words about my husband always be uplifting that I realized how horrible it is to sit around with women and discuss our husbands' failings.

Even if our husbands aren't within earshot of what we are saying, such talk places further doubt in our hearts that we have married the right person. And the more doubt we have, the more we look at everything he does with an attitude that says, "If I had only married the right person, then these situations wouldn't be happening." Before we know it, we're entertaining thoughts of leaving. We may even be searching for the one we "should" have married.

There are many Christians who were not walking with the Lord when they were married. Steve and I certainly weren't. What bothers me is those who claim that, because they did not marry as Christians, they do not have any obligation to stay with their spouse. God, they say, would have chosen them a different lifelong partner.

What a sad commentary on the state of marriage in our church today.

We must keep these thoughts out of our heads, and keep the words from leaving our lips.

So what do we do? Obviously, not one of us is married to the perfect husband.

I have set up a few guidelines for myself. One of them is that I will not talk negatively about my husband with other people. Because I am an imperfect being, I do sometimes get caught up in husband bashing. But I try hard not to do that. Another guideline is that, if there is a matter that I really am requesting people pray about, then I must have already been willing to spend the time on my knees before God prior to bringing it up with others. If I don't think it's worth the time on my knees, then I'd better not be telling others to get on theirs for me.

Only if Steve has given me permission to share certain aspects of our life together, and only if it is profitable, allowing someone to see that indeed the Lord can come in and change a situation, am I then free to share some of the "problems" that we have had in our marriage.

But we still have this need to tell someone what we are going through. Who do we tell?

Tell God! He is always there. He is always willing to listen. The best thing is that He is the only one who can really help. Sometimes, He helps by changing the person who is praying, not the husband she is praying for.

At some point in my walk with the Lord, I was desperately searching for perfection. What a surprise! The only way I knew to find perfection was in behavior. Therefore, I began to change my behavior to model what I thought the "perfect" Christian should be, do, say, and look like. As I changed nearly everything about myself, I decided that I wasn't the only one who needed to change. Steve must also change. I couldn't be a "perfect" Christian if my husband wasn't in the same place of holiness that I was, now could I?

I began to pray for the Lord to come in and minister to my husband. I may have even used the word "change." I no longer saw Steve when I looked at him. I saw a person who desperately needed to change his ways. I saw only a need for him to surrender all that he was to the Lord.

All of this is well and good, except for one minor thing, which actually became a major issue for me. I was not looking at Steve lovingly, or as a child of God who could hear from his heavenly Father on his own. I was looking at Steve with critical eyes and a critical heart. I was being his judge and jury, convicting him of every misdemeanor that I saw. Everything he did, I turned into a prayer. And all the time, I thought I was being holy. After all, I was praying for my husband frequently. Isn't that what wives are supposed to do?

I prayed, fully expecting that God would change my husband. I expected that, right before my eyes, he would move closer to the "holy now" side of the line. So I watched him with eagle eyes. And I was disappointed. Instead of seeing movement along the line toward holiness, I saw him backsliding.

How could he backslide? I was praying for him! God was supposed to make him into a great, holy Christian.

I became more fervent. I became more watchful. I became his Holy Spirit for him. As I prayed for every little thing he did wrong, I would begin to share with him all the areas in which the Lord was convicting him.

My "holy now" crusade was destructive both to our marriage and to Steve's walk with the Lord.

Unfortunately, I did not have the benefit many wise friends who could have shown me what I was actually doing to my husband. I had to rely on the Lord to change me, and show me where I was failing.

As I was praying for Steve, the Lord began to convict me of my own sin. I was reminded of the dear friend who shared with me that she never talks negatively about her husband. Initially, I felt that this reminder, coming in the middle of my prayers, was out of place. "I'm not talking negatively about my husband to anyone," I protested.

Then it hit me! Don't you hate those spiritual whammies? But this particular hit, although painful to my ego, was extremely good for my marriage. As I prayed on, I realized I was watching my husband so closely that I didn't have a chance to see the big picture. My watchfulness, I saw, was to the point that I was trying to take over the Lord's job in getting my husband to change.

Did I think that the Lord was clueless? Did I think that He couldn't talk to my husband? Or did I really think that if He did talk to Steve, that he wouldn't change? Somehow, I had turned Steve into my personal "holiness" project, dragging him along with me on my holiness quest.

In the end, I realized that there is no such thing as a "holiness quest." The Lord sanctifies us daily as we walk with Him. It's not up to us to pull our loved ones along behind us. The Lord leads them Himself on the same path.

Of course, I'm not saying it is wrong to pray for our husbands. But when we spend all our time focusing on what is wrong, we often miss what is right.

For a while after this experience, I had to do a total about face in prayer. I prayed for God to show me where Steve's strengths lie, and asked Him to bless Steve as He used those strengths to serve God.

So, you see, it wasn't Steve who was changed because of my prayers for him. I was the one God worked on.

"Let nothing be done through selfish ambition or conceit, but in lowliness of mind let each esteem others better than himself" (Philippians 2:3).

16
The Refuge

Several years ago I read a book, *The Spirit of Loveliness,* by Emilie Barnes. It was a marvelous book, even though while reading it I discovered I was not likely ever to be able to have a home environment as lovely as Emilie describes. However, all was not lost. I decided to implement one area of change in my life.

Steve was in a high-stress job at the time. He often came home grouchy and in a foul mood. He didn't seem to get much better as the evening wore on. He would have to deal with loud children, a floor littered with toys, not to mention a wife who was just plain sick of it all. Often he would retire to our bedroom after a long day at work, and take a nap.

I was resentful of his nap. I was the one who was tired. I was the one who had to deal with the children all day long. I was the one who was often woken up in the night. When Steve got home, I wanted him to take over, not take a nap.

I began to pray about Steve's naptime. Surely the Lord thought a nap after work was not productive. Surely the Lord would change Steve, and make him see that I was the one who really needed to be able to nap when he arrived home from work. Surely this was a character issue. The Lord definitely needed me to inform Him of my husband's bad behavior.

We all know that, when we start complaining to the Lord, He often changes our own hearts. In her book, Emilie wrote something that stuck me right to the core. She said: "A welcoming home is a place of refuge, a place where people worn down by the noise and turmoil and hostility of the outside world can find a safe resting place. A welcoming home is a place that you and others enjoy coming home to."*

This point really hit home with me. Was I making my home a resting place for my husband? Or was I taking all my frustrations of the day and piling them on his head as he walked in the door? There wasn't any place for him to go, when he arrived home, that was welcoming to him.

Later in the book, Emilie talks about the bedroom. She says that the bedroom should be the first priority in the home. What? I had never heard such a thing before. I didn't even make the bed. What was the point? We were just going to get back into it that night anyway. As I thought about what Emilie was conveying to my spirit, I realized the bedroom was the first place Steve headed for when he arrived home each evening.

Each evening his routine was the same: kiss the children, kiss the wife, look around, and then head up the stairs to change his clothes. I'm sure there were many days he sighed with frustration as he ascended the stairs to the master bedroom. There he would find a room full of dirty clothes, mixed with clean clothes, and a disheveled bed. As he made his way to the master bath, he would find the counter littered with toothbrushes, toothpaste, a curling iron that was used three months ago when we went on a date, towels, shampoo, a razor…Going into the toilet room, he was certain to come across an empty roll of toilet paper, magazines strewn about, and possibly even big hair balls that I removed from my brush while brushing my hair while sitting in the little toilet room. It's no wonder he wanted to shut it all out and take a nap.

As I read, I felt a real need to change things. Steve needed to be able to come home to a sanctuary. And I wasn't providing that for him.

I decided to begin by changing our bedroom. The next morning I cleaned and cleaned. However, that wasn't going to have a long-term effect. I needed to change myself in order to provide a sanctuary for my husband. I decided then and there that I would do at least a couple of things faithfully, including putting a fresh roll of toilet paper on the roll whenever it was empty. I also determined to put away my toothbrush and toothpaste after I used them. How hard can it be to replace a cap and put it into the drawer? The third and final change was to make the bed. I was going to make the bed every single morning, rain or shine. Our bedroom was going to be a refuge for my husband.

The only problem I encountered was the feeling that, if the bedroom became a refuge, then he would spend all of his evenings in there.

Because I set for myself three very definite goals, I was able to manage the change. If I had said to myself that I was going to keep my bedroom clean at all costs, that would have been completely unrealistic, and would have resulted in me feeling more defeated than ever.

Even now my bedroom might be trashed, but my bed will be made, there will never be an empty toilet paper roll on the dispenser (unless we've run out of toilet paper), and my toothpaste and toothbrush will be in their proper places. It's been about eight years. I wonder if I should add a couple more things to my list?

Remember my prayer that God would speak to Steve about his naptime? Well, you know what happened? I decided to change my heart. I made a conscious effort to not get upset about the nap every day. In fact, I decided to schedule a nap for myself every afternoon. About an hour and a half before Steve was to come home, all the kids and I would lie down for a nap. When Steve walked in the door, I was refreshed. You know, kisses from a refreshed wife are much better than those from a frazzled wife.

PART FOUR:
PERFECT LOVE

17
Getting to Know You

I often go a little overboard in trying to figure out Steve. I like to read all the marriage books. One thing that I had wanted to do was go to a marriage conference. I kept hearing how great they were. It wasn't that I felt my marriage was in jeopardy. But I look at marriage as something to be worked at, not taken for granted. Every time a marriage conference was in our area, I bugged Steve, and begged him, "Please, can't we go?" He always responded that he really didn't want to attend the conference.

I couldn't understand why he didn't want to go. After all, how many times in our marriage have we been able to get away without children for two whole nights? Not very many, I can assure you. To me, getting away for a couple of days sounded like paradise. We would have the added benefit of attending two days worth of seminars on how he could be a better husband. What could possibly be wrong with that?

That was actually how I felt. I didn't think there was anything I needed to do to change. Steve was the one with the problems.

I don't think I would have wanted to go to a marriage conference if that was how my spouse felt. Is it possible he could feel that attitude, coming through in my desire to go?

Whenever I brought up the subject, he would say something like, "Why? Our marriage is fine."

But I didn't want a fine marriage. I wanted a "perfect" marriage. And if I was going to get that, then Steve needed to go to the conference. So I pushed and pushed. Finally, the opportunity presented itself. A dear relative of mine, and her husband, were having marital difficulties. Steve agreed that we could take them to a marriage conference.

In the end, we weren't able to take them. However, my relative did end up going to a family life conference, and it was a pivotal point for their marriage. After hearing that, Steve was at last willing to go.

In spite of my attitude, we had a great time. I think I'm the one who got the most out of the conference. I learned many things about Steve that I hadn't really acknowledged before then.

One of these was something Steve said on the Sunday morning after the seminar. He told me, "Boy, I didn't even get a weekend."

I felt deflated. What did he mean? We had just spent a great three days and two nights together. Then I realized that, to him, a weekend means being at home relaxing. If he spends the time going places and doing things, then he feels he didn't get a weekend. I am just the opposite. If I am at home doing the same old stuff, then I feel I have lost out on a weekend.

Every Friday, the kids tell Steve, "Happy weekend!"

And I always think, "What's a weekend?" I often felt resentful that he got time off work, while my work continued day in, day out, seven days a week. I began to use the weekends to do my running-around things. I would leave all the kids at home, and go shopping, or to the library. At first, I felt guilty about it. But then I realized that it didn't matter to Steve having all the kids at home with him. As long as he didn't have to do the running around himself, he was fine.

It's sad how often we wives get resentful of our husbands. I went through a stage when I felt resentment about almost everything Steve was able to do by himself around the house. He could actually go into the bathroom, and shower, or do whatever he needed to do, and no one knocked on the door or disturbed him. I didn't understand that. How come the kids always knock on the door when I'm in the bathroom? Or he could spend an hour in the kitchen, and no one would ask him for a drink, or a cookie, or ask him to read to them. I walk into the kitchen and I'm followed by numerous children requesting my assistance. Steve can play on the computer for hours and not once be asked to do anything. As soon as I sit down at my computer, the requests come.

I know I shouldn't be resentful of those things. What they mean, more often than not, is that I am the one who meets the needs of my children. But sometimes I want them to need someone else.

One thing I learned much about at the marriage conference was meeting someone else's needs. Not the physical needs, but the "love language" needs. Gary Chapman's book, *The Five Love Languages*, had a powerful influence on me. I recommend it to everyone who wants to learn how to communicate love. Chapman's book discusses not only how to give love, but how love is received. If you read it, you will discover for yourself how much better your marriage can be when you are communicating love in a way that your spouse can hear.

In Dr. Chapman's view, there are five love languages: acts of service, gifts, quality time, words of affirmation, and physical touch. I love how he talks about the filling of the "love tank." When I speak my spouse's love language, his tank is full. But if I am speaking a different language, his tank is empty. Sure, I love my spouse, but he may not know it, because I do not communicate in his love language.

After reading the book, I was able to recognize that my love language is "words of affirmation." I like Steve to tell me that I am great. I like it even better if he tells me I am perfect. I know I'm not perfect, but I want him to tell me that I am. Sounds a bit egotistical, doesn't it? Even though it is my love language, I still feel that I could not say to my husband, "Please tell me I'm great."

I actually had a difficult time trying to figure out my love language. I seemed to fit many categories. I like to give gifts to people for no reason whatsoever. I like to spend quality time with Steve. I even like holding his hand. To me, all of those things say, "I love you." But my "love tank" doesn't empty if those things aren't done. The only time my tank feels empty is if the majority of the words coming out of Steve's mouth are negative.

When I first heard the concept of the five love languages, I was certain right off the bat that Steve's language was physical touch. As I explored this deeper, I realized his love language is actually "quality time." He wants to spend time with me. We don't have to say anything to each other, but we must be within a certain vicinity of one another. When I am gone from home, his tank gets empty. If I am around the house, his tank remains full.

I used to have my computer in my bedroom. I could then go behind my door, lock it, and not be disturbed by anyone. But I realized Steve's tank was getting empty. When I moved my computer into the office, within an easy roll of the desk chair from his computer, his tank filled up.

If we are doing separate activities around the house, he would rather I do my activity near him. If I want to read a book and he wants to watch the History Channel, he would rather I sit in a chair in the living room with him than go into another room to read. Even if our "quality time" is merely "nearby time," for him that is better than having an empty tank.

I also have a love language need for "quality time." One of the ways I like to get that is by going for a drive.

When I was a youngster, my mom and I used to drive around for hours, just talking. I remember one night, as we were driving around the city, we suddenly saw flashing red lights in the rearview mirror. A police officer came to our car window and asked my mom to get out. I began laughing hysterically. The officer gave me a stern look that caused me to laugh even more.

Mom returned to the car after having had to do all the sobriety tests. It appears that she had swerved a bit in her lane while we were talking and laughing with each other. She did not get a ticket, but the memory has stayed with us for a long time.

Even now, if we need to have a good talk, we get in a car and drive someplace.

I said earlier that, when Steve and I were dating, I often wanted to drive two hours to Los Angeles for pizza. It wasn't because the best pizza in the world was in a little restaurant near Venice Beach, although that was a part of it. I really wanted to go so that we could talk in the car.

Marriage is so much better when we are communicating in the same language.

18
The WWW Syndrome

Even though I want to greet Steve with a loving, passionate kiss each day when he arrives home, there are some days that I just can't seem to get it all together.

This was one of those days. I wasn't feeling well. If I had a real job I would have called in sick. But there is no calling in sick when you have eight children. Besides, it was our cleaning day. We missed it last week so we needed to work today.

I had gone to bed early the night before, but that didn't help me feel any better by morning. So I began the day later than usual, staying under my covers until I could no longer stand the sounds coming from the children. They all echoed in my mind as one cry: "We need our mommy."

After lying in bed for a few more minutes, hoping that someone would show up at the door to tend to my brood, I finally dragged my sorry body out of bed and down the stairs. The children were all playing. That would be fine except it was Thursday. Cleaning morning. Obviously they had all forgotten, even though the schedule was placed in a prominent place on the refrigerator. Even the older kids seemed to have forgotten, until they saw the look on my face.

I decided that, in spite of feeling crummy, I was still going to have a good day, and get a lot of work done. However, after the tenth time telling son John that he needed to pile all his things neatly before he put them away, I suddenly became transformed into the WWW.

In case you think, in this age of computers, that I was transformed into the World Wide Web and suddenly shot through the information superhighway at rapid speed, you are mistaken. What I became was the Wicked Witch of the West. My head began to throb as I ranted and raged. I should have found a pointed hat to go with the broom I was wielding, but I wasn't thinking clearly enough to grab a hat.

How did I solve my WWW problem? I went to take a nap, and hoped that the children would figure it out and get the living room cleaned up by themselves.

They didn't. Thirty minutes later, it looked the same.

Steve had wanted spaghetti for a few days, so I set out to make the noodles. All at once, the kids rallied and got the living room done. While the noodles were drying, I decided I could finally vacuum.

The more I vacuumed the more irritated I became. My crew of little "cleaner-uppers" had hidden things behind chairs and couches instead of putting them away. Then Bryan, who was in the midst of his potty training, decided it was time to go, which he did, right on the carpet in the bathroom. I cleaned it up, but it began to bring the WWW back into my attitude.

I left the room to see if I could straighten my attitude out. Back in the kitchen, I became furious. Erica was digging her hands in the bucket of wheat, spilling wheat berries on the floor, something she had already been disciplined for that day. And there were orange peels all over the counter and the kitchen floor.

Normally these are just minor irritations in life. But when the Wicked Witch of the West comes to visit, there is no stopping her.

As I put dinner on the table that evening, my grouchiness was evident to everyone. Even poor Steve had to stare down the WWW.

I decided the best thing would be for me to fly away on my broomstick. But even a broomstick could not stand up to the weather outside. There was nowhere to go, except to my room, for a good cry.

Instead, I decided there were a few people who had avoided my wrath. Perhaps I would leave after I had made everyone in the house miserable. Then I decided that there was no reason I should miss dinner. After all, I had made good whole-wheat spaghetti noodles. At least I could enjoy the meal.

There was silence around the table. Steve finally broke it by saying, "Everyone must love the dinner. You're all being so quiet." Suddenly the table erupted with compliments about the food, and all I do to help the family, and how sorry they were that they didn't do much to help out.

Remember how, in the Wizard of Oz, the one thing that could kill the witch was water? Well, in my house, the one thing that can kill the Wicked Witch of the West is compliments. I don't need a lot of "I'm sorrys," although that does help. What I really need is someone to make me feel I'm appreciated, even if I am sick.

Sometimes I think the best part of having a husband who knows me better than I know myself is that he knows what I need for my cure, even when I don't.

19
Just a Tad Distracted

Even though I still enjoy driving with Steve, we don't always see eye to eye on the rules of the road.

It's a proven fact that women are better drivers than men. Of course, I do not have any data to support this, but I know it to be true. Steve thinks the opposite on this important issue.

I am certain that I am the better driver in the family. And if you were to ask my children, they would all most certainly agree with me, especially the girls.

Our oldest daughter, Ashley, recently got her learners' permit. I took her into her dad's office and told him I was going to let her drive home. "No," he said. "I would like to give her some lessons first." She was disappointed. But it reinforced to me that he thinks I'm inadequate to teach her how to drive.

When we drive together, he is the one who gets honked at. Except, of course, if I'm driving while talking. Then I will occasionally drift into oncoming traffic, but I quickly correct myself. And there was the time I was reading a map, and looked up just in time to see that I was heading into the ditch, on the opposite side of the road. But those were just two small incidents. Nothing actually happened.

I often feel that the highway patrol guys tend to have their radar tuned to women. Steve drives fast all the time. I only remember him being pulled over on one occasion. And then, he got off with only a warning.

On the other hand, I stick close to the speed limit. Most of the time. It does seem that, whenever I'm deep in conversation, or there's a great song on the radio, I can find myself sometimes going just a tad too fast. Almost every time I've noticed myself going too fast, the highway patrol is right there. They have to be out to get me. I'm the only person I know who has been stopped five times in five years. We have a friend who typically drives eighty miles an hour, and he never gets ticketed.

I once told the kids that perhaps, if I saved up enough tickets, I would get a free trip somewhere. One of them piped up, "Yeah. To jail!"

Even sitting here at my computer, I'm shaking my head at the whole situation. I wonder if I should move to Montana, where they only fine you for wasting gas if you drive too fast.

Of course, I am the first to admit that I should be given a speeding ticket if I deserve it.

On my birthday, I drove Ashley over to a friend's house. I was just minding my own business, chatting away with her, when I looked at the speedometer and realized I was going way too fast. As I eased up on the gas pedal, I saw a highway patrol officer in front of me, and knew I was in for it.

I quickly pulled over to the side of the road, and waited for him to turn around at the next intersection. There was no reason to make him come after me. I knew I was speeding. Many thoughts raced (maybe that's not a good choice of word?) through my mind.

I didn't want a ticket. But I deserved a ticket. What message would this send to my daughter with her new permit?

I decided I would take my ticket without whining, and pay my debt to society. No excuses. I would simply own up to what I had done and take my punishment.

Handing the officer my license and registration, without him even asking for them, I casually mentioned that all the information was correct, including the date of birth.

He returned to my window several minutes later. As he handed me his ticket book to sign he said, "I'm just giving you a warning. Happy birthday. And you might want to slow down if you want to live to the next one."

Whew!

No! I need a ticket! I deserve a ticket! I was speeding! I should be taught a lesson! Of course I didn't demand a ticket. I thanked the officer, signed the warning, and, slowly, drove away.

I relayed this story to my dad when he phoned to wish me a happy birthday, and he relayed his own story about getting pulled over for speeding. It hadn't been on his birthday, and he did demand a ticket.

I felt even worse. If I were a decent human being, I would have demanded that justice be served. I would have demanded my ticket. I would have paid the huge fine, and had my insurance increase. I would have demanded my rights as a law-breaking citizen! But, I'm a wimp.

I am so glad I don't get what I deserve from God. I'm delighted that He doesn't write me a ticket for everything I've ever done. Now as I sit here, I can see him hanging on the cross, bearing the burden of my speeding, of my lack of thought for the law. He is not begging for mercy. He is demanding that He be given all the punishment that I deserve. He is demanding that the sins of the entire world be placed on His shoulders. All

I have to do is ask Him, and he will take away all of my sins. Even if it isn't my birthday.

Speeding is one thing, but accidents are quite another thing altogether.

I am grateful that I don't get into accidents. Some people truly are accident-prone. I can't remember having a car accident since I've been married. I don't, of course, count the time that I backed into the tree. I was in someone's driveway, and one of my kids yelled, "Watch out!" I looked up and saw a tractor, going about five miles an hour, at least three miles away. I was a bit disgusted by my son's lack of faith in my ability to see danger. So, just a bit more quickly than I normally would have, I put my foot on the gas. And bang! We hit the tree.

"What was that?" I inquired. One of the kids filled me in. I got out and surveyed the damage. Nothing broken but a small red light. When I got back into the car, I mentioned to the children that it really wasn't that big of a deal to hit the tree.

That was when the kids began talking about the time I was blinded by the sun and ran through a red light, so that all the traffic in every direction had to stop. We used that experience to talk about how God often will protect us from danger. See? It wasn't an accident. It was a learning experience.

A couple of times, I have seen accidents in my rearview mirror. I was so glad the Lord protected me, when I was only seconds from being involved.

At least I didn't have anything to do with causing them.

That did happen once to a friend. She was driving along, minding her own business. When she glanced into her rearview mirror, she saw that a truck containing barbeque sauce had tipped over on its side. She went back to see if she could help. When she got to the scene of the accident, the truck driver pointed to her and said, "It was her fault." She stills claims it had nothing to do with her. I think

I would too. Who wants to be known forever as the woman who caused the road to be plastered with barbeque sauce?

When Steve and I ride together in the car, he always drives. He makes me nervous when I drive. He is always saying things like, "You're too close to the curb!" "How fast are you going?" "Turn on your blinker." "Lights!"

So you can see why I was a bit nervous about the idea of Steve teaching Ashley to drive. He will make her nervous, and will think she is a rotten driver if she happens to go over the curb a few times while making right turns. As long as there aren't any people on the sidewalk, I don't see why that should matter. I use it all the time.

As soon as Steve gives her a few lessons, I'm looking forward to riding in the passenger seat like a true passenger…with knuckles white from gripping the door.

20
White Knuckle Moments

I have had several "white knuckle moments" in my life. Shortly after I had Christi, I decided that it would be "cool" to be an actress or a model. As I am just shy of five foot two, being a fashion model was definitely out of the question, so I decided to try being an actress. Of course, that doesn't mean just popping into a studio somewhere and saying, "I'm here!" First, I had to find ways to get "noticed." We only lived a couple of hours from Los Angeles, so occasionally I got a babysitter and headed down the hill to seek fame and fortune.

One project I participated in was a haircutting demonstration. I then had to go back to Los Angeles to do a photo shoot. This was held in the evening, and lasted until almost two in the morning. On the way home, I could not find my way back to the freeway. Suddenly, I discovered that I was in an area of the city that was not known for its great hospitality. Everywhere I looked, throngs of people crowded the sidewalks. There were bars on all the windows and doors. Fear engulfed me, fear for my life. I locked all the car doors and continued driving.

Then terror struck. The light ahead was red.

I am not the type of person who purposefully breaks the law. But I was terrified of stopping my car. This qualified as a "white knuckle" moment. An inner struggle with my conscience went on before I decided not to hit the brakes. I went right through the red light, then through the next one. At that moment, it was worth the cost of a ticket if I could get directions to the freeway. I began to pray out loud. "Lord, please, get me out of here!"

Just then, I saw two police cars in a parking lot. I pulled up to them, rolled down my window and, with tears in my eyes, said, "How do I get on the freeway?"

The officer kindly gave me the directions.

"Do you mind," I asked him, "if I don't stop at the red lights?"

He said, "Feel free to go right through, Ma'am."

About an hour after I finally got on the freeway, I realized that I was still gripping the steering wheel with white knuckles. Even though I was out of danger, fear was still in my heart. I had to ask the Lord to deliver me from the fear. I also had to repent for not immediately trusting Him. Trusting the Lord is not always easy when we are faced with fear.

Another "white knuckle" moment occurred when I was shopping at a grocery store. I turned to go into the next aisle and was paralyzed with fear. Three young men were standing there. It appeared to me there was a spiritual battle going on between us. My whole being began to shake. I felt that I was going to faint. You can only understand if you have experienced a moment like this. As I stood literally shaking in my boots, I suddenly felt the Lord come upon me, and whisper to me that He would keep me safe. I began to pray for the salvation of the three young men standing at the end of the aisle. The moment passed quickly, but I will not forget it as long as I live.

I began to realize that to fear for my life in any situation was ridiculous. After all, what was the worst thing that could happen? I would die. So what? It was in that "white knuckle" moment that the Lord taught me a huge lesson about fear.

When we fear for our lives, the fear that grips us is usually as fleeting as the danger. But what about the fears that seem to fill us as we go about the tasks that God has called us to do? How do we deal with the fears of everyday life?

When Ashley was three years old, Steve and I decided we were going to homeschool her. That was not a decision that came without fear.

21
Freedom from Fear

I'm truly glad that confidence is not a prerequisite to setting out on the journey of homeschooling. If it were, few families would take the plunge. Almost all those I have talked to began their homeschooling journey wondering why God would call them to do something that terrified them so much. It didn't help that most of their relatives, friends, and fellow church members doubted they could pull it off. I'm sure we had relatives who were hoping we would quickly come to our senses and put the children in school, where they belonged.

Most of us, as we begin our first year of homeschooling, feel that we are under a microscope. Relatives begin "testing" our children's knowledge. Well-meaning friends wonder when the kids will begin exhibiting "social reject" tendencies. A naturally shy child, who has always been shy, is suddenly considered "unsocialized." A naturally outgoing child, who has always been outgoing, now needs more of the "right" kind of social interaction.

After the third week of homeschooling, we wonder if we have made a mistake. Little Suzie still isn't reading the King James Version. In fact, she can't even remember the sound the letter "d" makes, even though we have covered it every day for the past three weeks. And we thought she would have superior knowledge, from being homeschooled! Meanwhile, the house has fallen apart. The little children begin showing signs of rebellion. Our husband comes home to find us worn out and exhausted. Who wouldn't be exhausted doing five hours of school with a five-year-old? He too begins to wonder about the wisdom of homeschooling our children. The fear that we had in the beginning is getting stronger.

Then something wonderful happens. We go to our first Mom's Night Out meeting. Or perhaps we venture into a homeschool chat room. We meet other homeschooling moms. We cry out to them that we are scared. We don't think we can do this job. We don't even LIKE doing this job. The women turn us to face God. He has called us to this job; He will give us the strength, and even the courage, to perform the tasks that He requires of us. We learn to seek Him first.

There have been several times in my life when I've questioned if God has really called me, or if I was just trying to keep my kids home so I would have someone to play with all day.

I know that homeschooling my children is what is best for our family. But there are times when seeds of doubt come pouring in on me. So what do I do when I feel the urge to stick my thumb out the next time the yellow school bus is passing my house? First of all I realize that I could not possibly have all of my children ready to get onto the bus at such an early hour. Then I realize that the bus doesn't take three-year-olds.

It's always easier to convince myself of something if it will be the easiest option for me. So I sit down and think about how much harder it would be to send my kids to school. There would be at least one day each week that a child would forget his lunch, so I would have to get in the car and drive twenty miles to the school to deliver a peanut butter and jelly (not again, Mom!) sandwich, fruit, and boxed drink.

Then there would be all the after-school activities that I would have to attend. Practices and rehearsals. There would be kids who missed the bus because they were going to the bathroom. Kids who got sick in the middle of the day.

All of those things would upset the delicate balance I would set up for myself if my kids were in school. I would have my schedule all worked out. I would clean the house every morning, and it would remain that way all day, as I watched soaps, tread on the treadmill, took hot baths, read good books, chatted on the Internet, talked on the phone, and spent time ministering to mothers of young children.

Hey! Wait a minute. Am I supposed to be convincing myself NOT to send my kids to school?

The days I look longingly for the bus to stop are days that I am stressed out. Those are the days that I think I can't make it one more day! Those are the days I want someone to come and take away all the children so I can get my house clean.

Those are the days that send me back to my Savior.

God often gives us different reasons to homeschool our children. I firmly believe He convicts us and expects us to follow through, even if it's painful at times. I have never known Him to require only the easy things out of me. In fact, I marvel at how often He calls me to do something that I know I'm not capable of doing. But when I turn to Him, He equips me for the task.

If I let the stressed-out days get me down, then what does that say about my character? It says I'm wishy-washy and don't believe in my convictions. Sometimes, when I'm feeling particularly stressed, I need to sit down, prayer in my heart, and pen in my hand. I have to ask the Lord to remind me why I'm doing this. As I pray and am reminded, I often need to write out my reasons for homeschooling, so that, when I'm gripped with fear, or when I look longingly for the bus to pull up next to the driveway, I'm more prepared to not stick out my thumb for a ride.

Homeschooling allows us to take breaks to suit our family. Steve's job is busiest in the summer, so it's much easier for him to take time off for a vacation at other times of the year. The "Camp" school goes into slow motion in the summer, but we still do some math, reading, and writing each day, which means we don't have to spend long periods in review each September, as do most regular school classes.

After evaluating the benefits and the demands, we have chosen to not put our children into organized sports. With a large family, the time commitment needed for practices and games would be too much for us. But our children are involved in the 4H Club, which is very busy in the summer, and our oldest daughters raise and train Arabian horses. All these activities are part of their schooling, and allow for a healthy amount of social interaction with a wide range of ages.

As significant as these aspects of homeschooling are, the most important motive for our decision is expressed in God's command to his people in Deuteronomy 6:6-9, which says: "And these words which I command you today shall be in your heart. You shall teach them diligently to your children, and shall talk of them when you sit in your house, when you walk by the way, when you lie down, and when you rise up. You shall bind them as a sign on your hand, and they shall be as frontlets between your eyes. You shall write them on the doorposts of your house and on your gates."

When I first came across this passage, I wondered how I could possibly obey God's commands for my family if my children were away from me for the largest portion of my day. How could I spend the time when they lie down, when they rise up, when we sit, and when we walk? When would we actually get to do that?

As Steve and I prayed about desiring to homeschool our children, we were bombarded with reasons why we should do it. Everywhere we turned, we seemed to run into homeschoolers. I was even watching a preacher on television when he began talking about homeschooling. Steve and I were convinced the Lord was telling us to homeschool our children.

Making the decision was the easiest part. Fear of failure had to be dealt with later. It takes a while to feel comfortable homeschooling your children.

The scenario goes something like this:

We learn that we don't have to spend five hours a day schooling a five-year-old, and we begin to relax.

THEN, the five-year-old grows. We have more children to homeschool. We fear that we will not be able to answer all the children's needs. Once again, the search begins for the "perfect" curriculum for our growing requirements. We may find it, or we may not, but we question. We are always questioning our ability to homeschool.

THEN, it is time for HIGH SCHOOL! Again we are gripped with fear. How can I help with advanced science? What if I don't get it, and can't help when my child comes to me and says, "Mom, I don't get it"?

"There is no fear in love; but perfect love casts out fear, because fear involves torment. But he who fears has not been made perfect in love. We love Him because He first loved us" (1 John 4:18,19).

Satan likes to plant seeds of fear in our lives. Fear makes us ineffective, and turns us away from God, into ourselves. If we fear not being able to find the "perfect" curriculum, we are searching ONLY for that. We forget to ask God what He wants for our children.

Whenever fear embraces me, I need to remember that if I turn to Jesus, He will answer my fear. He will show me the way that I am to walk. He will also help me by guiding me to people with the answers I need, like the mom who told me, "Relax, have fun, and enjoy your children the way you used to when you taught them everything else in life."

22
Pivotal Moment

I love it when the Lord comes to me and changes the direction I am going. I refer to these many times in my life as "pivotal" moments. Often these pivotal moments have to do with my husband. One such moment occurred not long ago.

We were alone in the car together, coming home from a movie. Suddenly, I was overcome with a pivotal moment. As we sat in silence, the Lord spoke to my heart. You know how they say that, when you are about to die, your life flashes before your eyes? Well, in that moment, my love for Steve flashed before my heart. God somehow took my feelings for my husband over the past fifteen years, and compressed them into one lump moment.

Can you imagine fifteen years of emotion, balled up into one moment and thrust into your heart? My eyes filled with tears. I had been married to this man for fifteen years, but never had I KNOWN beyond a shadow of a doubt that it was forever! I had often felt that perhaps there would be a way out for me. I don't know why, but I always held onto the idea that, if I wasn't happy with the way things were going, then I could bail out.

But on this particular evening, that all changed. I knew, in that pivotal moment, that this marriage is for a lifetime. That one realization changed my focus. If this is for a lifetime, then why am I selfish? If this is for a lifetime, then why don't I always give my all? If this is for a lifetime, then why am I holding on to thoughts that don't belong in my heart? If this is for a lifetime, then why don't I behave as though this man sitting next to me is my life?

All these questions flooded through me in that brief time. My tears continued to fall in the darkness of the car. Steve was lost in his own world of thought, unaware of my thoughts and feelings.

Images of my life with Steve began to flash before my eyes. I actually wondered if we were going to die. But that was not the Lord's intention. I believe His intention was to turn me from where I was going and head me on to a better path, a path of unconditional love toward my husband. I saw in my mind's eye several scenes of Steve being emptied of himself, and showing only his love for me. I can't explain how I knew that he was emptied, but I knew. As I watched the vision, I realized there were not any pictures of me with that same attitude. The Lord was trying to tell me something.

I did not love my husband unconditionally. There was always something in me that held back the unconditional part. I still felt that Steve could do something that would allow me not to love him anymore. But that is not what God demands of me. I am to love him in the same way that Jesus loves me. I am to love him with a heart of acceptance, of love, and forgiveness, no matter what! There aren't any other options. Jesus died on the cross for the sins that I had not yet committed. He knew that I would commit them and would need to be redeemed. In that same way, I must, knowing that Steve will sin, forgive him for those things that I do not yet know.

23
Change Can Be Painful

I have mentioned before that I am a non-confrontational type of person. Some of the people who know me may not agree, because I can debate with the best of them. But that is not what I'm referring to here. What I mean is that I will run a mile rather than bring up an issue that will be either painful, or embarrassing, to me, or to the other party.

In some ways, this is fine. I don't go around hurting people's feelings. But, in a marriage relationship, it is good to be able to share and discuss these intimate issues with your spouse. That is part of what it means to love unconditionally.

Steve has given me permission to share this story with you. (He also has full editorial rights.)

Before we were married, Steve had become entrapped by sin. I knew this, but did not fully grasp the hold that this particular sin can have on a person. I pretty much figured that, once we were married, he wouldn't have a need for it anymore.

After we were married, I discovered that it was still a small part of his life. The pain was unbearable. But rather than share that with Steve, I kept my feelings hidden. At that point, I wasn't even willing to pray for him. I hardened my heart. I tried to pretend it was his problem and not mine.

A few years later, I thought that Steve had been delivered from the hold the sin had on him.

Several years passed before I discovered that he was once again caught in its grip. I can hardly describe the incredible pain that enveloped me. It was as if I had found out that my husband was having an affair.

The first thing I did was cry. I cried for hours. And then I cried out to God. "Why did you let him do this? Why haven't you stopped him? Why can't you make this pain go away?"

I knew that I was not going to be able to forgive Steve for this. I wasn't sure at that point if I could stay married to him. I felt as though he had cheated on me. And if my husband had an affair, then I could get out of the marriage.

I thought perhaps I could just leave him a note, and skip out quietly in the night.

I stayed with the Lord a long time that afternoon. Even though I know what I have to do, I don't always do it right off the bat. Finally, though, I felt myself surrender to the Lord. I was convinced that I had to tell Steve how I felt.

That night, I experienced an indescribable time of healing as Steve and I talked. I realized that if I had shared my feelings with him earlier, there was a possibility that much of the pain could have been prevented. I vowed to him that I would share with him how I felt. And he vowed that he would not hurt me again in that way.

Was the change in me lasting? Yes. Even though I occasionally drift back into the hold-my-feelings-in mode, I am quickly reminded that Steve is my forever friend. He is the man who was created to be with me. He is the one whose heart God has joined with mine. He is the one who will always be with me, until death do us part.

Peter felt the same way about Jesus. He was certain that he could never deny Jesus, yet within a few short hours, he had denied Him not once, but three times. When Peter was reminded of Jesus' words to him, telling him that he was going to deny Jesus, Peter went outside and wept bitterly.

Love for a spouse isn't something that conquers all sin. Peter sinned against the greatest friend anyone could ever have, one who was perfect. In our imperfection, we will all sin.

But what was Peter's response? He wept.

How could I possibly ever sin against the man that I love so desperately? Even though my desire is to never sin against him, and I know his desire is the same, we are still imperfect people in a sinful world. But there is hope because we can repent, weep bitterly, and be restored to a right relationship with each other.

24
Forgive My Selfishness

Something wasn't right between Steve and me. I was being too hardheaded and stubborn about it. I lay in bed, thinking about it, tears falling silently from my eyes, my whole body turned toward the wall and away from my husband.

Now, you'd think that I would have learned enough to make peace before I went to bed. The verse of Scripture that warns us not to let the sun go down on our anger (Ephesians 4:26) penetrated my heart. But still, I did nothing.

Steve and I could feel each other wrestling in our hearts. But selfishness won out. And I paid for that sinful stubbornness. The next day was totally and completely crummy.

The morning began with my normal kiss from Steve, and his usual, "Goodbye, I love you." But this "goodbye" was wrapped up in the unspoken words and feeling that said, "There is a chasm in our relationship." Every morning, Steve leaves me with that kiss and a "goodbye, I love you." Even in my sleep, I know that he does this. I don't always wake up when he leaves; sometimes I just sink down, comforted by knowing that he is going off to work so that I can stay beneath my warm comforter until the children wake up.

But not this day. There was no comfort for me. My heart ached. This was reflected immediately by my harried, hurried day, by all the things that began going wrong.

It is a dreadful feeling to know that you are being selfish, and still want to go on being selfish.

I had to run an errand in the car, and found myself longing to see Steve, to be able simply to tell him, "I'm sorry. Please forgive me." As I drove, deep in thought, I looked up to see him pass me in the other direction. I didn't even see him in time to wave at him. In turmoil, I wondered: *Does he think I am still angry with him? Is he still angry with me?* I watched him in my rearview mirror until he was out of sight.

I so longed to turn around and chase him down, but I knew that he was heading to the office for a meeting. Chasing him was not an option. Afterwards, I realized that it hadn't even been his truck. I had wanted to see him so much that I had imagined it.

When I got back home, I called his office. I knew he was in a meeting, but I hoped he would be able to come to the phone. No go. Then I waited on pins and needles for him to return my call. I chewed over in my mind what I should do. I thought of surprising him by taking him out to lunch.

The comforting thing was, I never doubted he would forgive me. In all the years we've been married, he has always forgiven me. More than once, he has had to forgive me for the same thing. Usually, it is my selfishness.

Steve's continual forgiveness has really helped me to understand the forgiveness of Jesus. Sometimes, I keep repeating the same sin, even though it is not what I desire to do. But Christ still forgives me. And doesn't He see our hearts? He knows we don't want to do what we do. When I do something that I know hurts Jesus, I long to seek His forgiveness. I long to tell Him, "I'm sorry." And I equally long for Him to say, "I forgive you."

The same thing goes for my husband. And every time I ask him to forgive me, he does.

Forgiveness is an awesome thing. It mends the hearts of those who are both needing to forgive and those needing the forgiveness.

Later that day, in the midst of cleaning the bathroom, I heard a sudden commotion, doors banging and children yelling. At first, I thought, "But I have to get this finished. I can't tend to them right now." That thought lasted all of thirty seconds. Another door banged shut. Quickly, I called the two perpetrators down. They sat on opposite sides of the room, glaring at each other. As soon as I walked in, they began. "He did this!" "She did that!" "She's so mean!" "No, I'm not. You're mean!"

Now it was my turn to talk. I told them to hush, then called them both to stand nose to nose in the middle of the room. (The thought crossed my mind that someone should have told Steve and me last night to turn nose to nose. It's so effective.) John stuck his tongue out at Briana. A tear dripped down Briana's face. As they stood there, I talked to them about forgiveness.

Within two minutes, I saw the change in their hearts. I saw in them a willingness to forgive, and to be forgiven. They looked at each other, embraced, and said in unison, "I love you. Please forgive me." Then John said, "Hey, want to play with me?" Their example was humbling. No doubt I needed to show the same change of heart to my husband.

25
Mrs. Noah: My Hero

When I was searching the Bible for the perfect wife to emulate, I came to Mrs. Noah. Surely she was perfect. If her husband was perfect, then she of course had to be perfect too.

Sometimes, I wonder if Mrs. Noah made the same mistakes in her marriage as I do. Do you think that, when Noah came home after his conversation with God about building the ark, that Mrs. Noah said to him, or even thought to herself, "You are insane"?

Through all the years when Noah was building the boat, do you think she ever harped on at him about working too hard, or not spending enough time with Ham, Shem, and Japheth?

Do you think she ever complained about doing all that laundry?

When they finally got on the ark, and the big door closed, do you think she got a little bit scared? Do you think she ever questioned God?

Even when the floods came and they began to float away, do you think she longed for her clean house back home?

I complain about all the cooking I have to do. But think of all the meals she had to prepare. I complain about one dirty diaper. Think of what it must have been like in the ark.

I really do think Mrs. Noah must have been perfect.

But for some reason, the Lord didn't want us to know much about her. Could it be that we would want to emulate her, rather than Him? Could it be that God, in His infinite wisdom, knew that we would want to look to a person for our example, so He didn't put anyone in the Bible who was perfectly upright and moral, without fault?

Noah was about as perfect a man as there was. Scripture tells us: "Noah was a just man, perfect in his generations. Noah walked with God" (Genesis 6:9b). But when you read further, you see that Noah got drunk and allowed his son to see his nakedness. I wonder how Mrs. Noah felt about that?

Do you think she felt like leaving Noah? Do you think she thought he dealt too harshly with Ham? Do you think she was mad as a hornet's nest?

I'm glad I don't know the answers to those questions. I would rather think that she forgave her husband. I would rather think that, somehow, God was changing her in the midst of all that she had to endure. Of course, we don't know what He was doing with her. Her story remains untold.

Yet, I think we can learn a lot from Mrs. Noah. She stayed by her man, even when the world laughed at him. She stayed by him when there must have been great fear of the unknown. We assume that she even stayed by him in his sin, after the flood. We don't know, because she isn't mentioned again. But the fact remains: we are descended from Noah and his wife. She is the mother of all people, and she doesn't even have a name.

But we can learn from her.

As wives, we are to follow our husbands wherever the call of the Lord leads them through life. A woman is to stay by her husband's side even if the world is laughing at him. And when he steps out onto the dry land that the Lord has provided, she is to be there to rejoice with him.

Mrs. Noah was a great woman!

I do want to be like Mrs. Noah. I have done my best to multiply and fill the earth. Our family has calculated that, if each of our children has eight children, and each of their children has eight children, then we will add two hundred and twelve people to the world, all in a matter of forty years. That's an awesome responsibility. I had better be certain that my children are grounded in Christ.

PART FIVE:
AND DAILY PERFORM MY VOWS

26
When My Heart Is Overwhelmed

There are times in my life when I get this feeling that I am not cutting the mustard. I will sit in my living room, look around at my children, and feel that I am totally failing them. At times like that, I focus on the external things. Erica has her shirt on backwards, or the back of her dress is tucked into the back of her underwear. Bryan has a saggy diaper, or the remains of a cookie still on his face. Briana somehow has managed to look like she had been through the dryer, and all her clothes are wrinkled. David is yelling at John to help him clean their room, which looks like a tornado detoured through it on the way to Kansas. John, of course, is rebelling against his older brother's authority, and simply sitting on his bed. Ashley might be checking her e-mail. Again! Christi is simply staring at the socks she is supposed to match. And Cathy is writing a letter, misspelling every third word.

It is in those moments that I think I am not good at this mom-of-eight-kids, book writing, homeschooling, husband-loving-wife job that God has called me to do. I cry out to Him, and beg Him to make me be the perfect "everyone" that I am supposed to be.

It is then that He opens my eyes to what is really before me. Scattered throughout the house are blessings that I cannot even count. You know the song that goes, "Count your blessings, name them one by one...see what God has done." The song does not say "see what I have done." It says "see what GOD has done." When He opens my eyes to see what He has done, how can I sit and think that I should give up any part of what He has done?

I can choose to stay slumped on the couch, looking at all that is going wrong in my life. I can see all the areas where I am failing, or think I might be failing. Or I can look at life through the eyes of God. What does God see in my life?

Does He see me as a failure? Does He judge me with an iron fist? Does He want me to stop any of the things that He has called me to do? Would He have called me to be a mom to eight children if He hadn't equipped me to do it? Would He have called me to homeschool those children if He hadn't equipped me to do it? Would He have called me to be a loving wife if He hadn't equipped me to do it?

Of course not.

You see, God didn't call me to be anything, or do anything, that He wasn't willing to equip me to do. That doesn't mean I will do everything perfectly. He is working with imperfect material. But when I am clinging to Him, looking to Him for wisdom and strength to do the tasks He has called me to do, then I cannot be a failure in His eyes.

When He called me to homeschool, I was terrified. But I clung to Him. Why would I stop clinging now? When we first decided to let God plan our family size, I was terrified. But I clung to Him. When I felt my marriage was falling apart, I clung to Him, and He restored my marriage.

Cling to Him! Look at your life through God's eyes. Pray to Him, to guide you in all that you do. Be ever willing to listen and obey.

"Hear my cry, O God; Attend to my prayer. From the end of the earth I will cry to You, When my heart is overwhelmed; Lead me to the rock that is higher than I. For you have been a shelter for me, A strong tower from the enemy. I will abide in Your tabernacle forever; I will trust in the shelter of Your wings. For You, O God, have heard my vows; You have given me the heritage of those who fear Your name. You will prolong the king's life, His years as many generations. He shall abide before God forever. Oh, prepare mercy and truth, which may preserve him! So I will sing praise to Your name forever, that I may daily perform my vows" (Psalm 61).

27
When Mom Loses It!

If you're still wondering how strongly I need to cling to the Savior, and have Him refocus my vision, I'll give you another glimpse into my life. Use your imagination, if you dare, to picture this scenario. I'm sure none of you could have anything like it in your own memory.

All of my children were delightfully doing their chores. At least, that is what I wanted them to be doing. Instead, I heard, from behind the closed bedroom door where the boys were supposed to be cleaning their room, "You're not cleaning."

"Why are you so mean?"

"Why are you so lazy?"

"Why do you wet the bed?"

"Why don't you clean up after yourself?"

As I listened, I began to wonder if they were going to work it out, or if they were going to make me stop what I was doing and tend to their argument.

Their disagreement escalated quickly. Within a minute, John was crying and screaming at his brother. I wish I could say that I calmly walked into the room and settled them down, praying with them, and joyfully showing them the next step they needed to take in their tasks. Unfortunately, that wasn't the reality of the moment.

I threw the book I was holding. I stomped into their room. When I saw that there had been not one iota of work done, I lost all sense of judgment. Instead of setting a good example for my children, I acted like the fool that the Bible warns me not to let my children be companions of. I behaved like an appalling maniac. I ranted and raged, and then stormed out of the room, slamming the door behind me.

The strange thing about this was that I didn't even feel remorse. What I felt was helplessness. My brain was hurting. I couldn't figure out why I was acting like a raving lunatic. Did I then and there repent of my actions? No, I didn't. I went back to cleaning the room we call "the library." It was a job that was overwhelming, even to a seasoned library "cleaner-upper" like me.

A home library is very important to me. Mine consists of wall-to-wall bookcases, filled with books categorized by topic. This obviously has gone unnoticed by most of the children in the house, who pull books off the shelves, then leave them lying on the floor. Worse yet, they will put a book on child training back in the section on animal behavior (or did I do that?).

The library, when it is clean, also becomes the favorite play spot in the house. If there is a floor anywhere that is not already littered with toys, the children will migrate to it, and do their best to ensure that it soon matches the rest of the floors in the house.

On this day, the floor of the library was not at all visible. Someone had gone in and cut up poster-board in order to make armor for all the young children in the house. In addition, there was a huge glue spill, scissors, many bits of paper, crayons, markers, and basically the entire animal collection in our house, all littering the library floor.

The shelves were also in a terrible state. There were books that someone had placed on the shelves sideways! Can you believe it? Now, a book placed on a shelf sideways is not normally cause for great alarm; however, when Mom is in a tizzy, anything can set her off, or keep her steaming mad. I'm certain puffs of smoke came from my ears as everything that was out of place was magnified in my mind.

As I worked, I listened to the seemingly endless spats and unkind conversations going on around my house. None of the children were getting along. At last, I gave up and went downstairs. The first thing I noticed was that the table had not been cleared after lunch. Squished-up blueberries and cherries littered the carpet. The table was covered with crumbled chips, spilled drinks, leftover food, and a few other things that didn't belong there in the first place, like the mail.

I lost it. Again. I yelled for everyone to get downstairs. NOW! The whole time my children worked at cleaning up, I barked at them about how lazy they were for not having done it sooner. I will spare you the horrible details. Just take my word for it: I will not get the mother of the year award for that episode.

Do you think I repented? NO! I was angry, and felt that I deserved to be angry. I was so hurtful to my children that it makes me well up with tears as I think about it now.

After that, I had one of my children carry a box of books from the library to the bookshelf downstairs. I heard the thud as she fell down the stairs. I managed to muster up a little bit of sympathy for her, but my thoughts went to what I saw on the stairs. There, on the sixth step up, was a huge pile of Lego. Again, I mustered the kids downstairs.

They thought I was angry before! My mind was racing. I kept thinking, "You can't talk like that to your children." Still I continued. Finally I ran out of the room, and up the stairs sobbing.

For the kids, life went on as usual.

When Steve got home, I informed him that I was in a really bad mood. I don't think he needed to be told. My snarl when he kissed me probably gave me away.

He responded that I needed a vacation. We were planning to leave in a few days for a three-week cross-country trip with all the kiddos. He was excited. I was thinking, "I'd rather die!"

It wasn't until dinner was over that I began to feel my brain stop hurting. I realized that I had really been angry for several days.

After the kids went to bed, I indulged in my favorite pastime. I logged on to the homeschool chat room on crosswalk.com. Several nights a week, after all the children are in bed, I will log on to speak with adults who often struggle with the same experiences as I do.

It was there that I found what I needed. A woman told us that her husband had died four years earlier, leaving her with seven children, eleven and under. She said she needed encouragement. But instead, she gave me a new heart. I told her about yelling at my husband because he wanted clean socks. She just wanted to have her husband back, so she *could* give him clean socks.

The next morning, once again, I assembled the troops. I had them all sit, and I told them how sorry I was for being so horrible and mean. Do you know what they did? Without even thinking about it, they said in unison, "We forgive you!" Then they began telling me all the reasons they felt they deserved my wrath. Quickly I told them that there is nothing they could do that would make me not love them. And I was so sorry that I had acted as though I didn't love them. I had tears in my eyes as the children all gave me a group kiss, and we were restored.

Aren't you glad God is forgiving? Aren't you glad that His acceptance of us isn't based on how we act?

28
Postpartum Reds

I know you are all familiar with the term "postpartum blues." Steve claims that the word blue is too nice to describe what happened to me. Around the third week after having a baby, I suddenly became a woman with one thing on her mind. RAGE!

I never knew quite how this started. I would be going along with life as usual, feeding the baby, changing the baby, feeding the baby, changing the baby...There wasn't much else to think about, except the needs of the baby.

Then, Steve would begin to think that perhaps I could begin getting myself back to normal. He would say something innocent enough, like, "Maybe we could have dinner tonight?" Or even, "I don't have any clean underwear. Do you think I could get some by tomorrow morning?"

Without warning, I would boil over the top, and spew my venom all over him. The scenario was the same every time. I screamed. I cried. I packed my bags. At that point, I would remember I couldn't leave, because I wasn't allowed to drive for six weeks after the C-section.

So there I was, with my clothes packed, ready to storm out in search of...

I don't know what I was in search of. All I knew was that I didn't want to have to deal with things like dinner and clean underwear.

A couple of times, when I didn't have C-section deliveries, I actually put my bags in the car and headed off to some unknown destination. I usually drove around the block. Once, I think I was gone for twenty whole minutes. Of course, by the time we had our third baby, Steve knew the routine. He didn't worry too much about me going off the deep end. He knew that it wouldn't take long for me to hit bottom, and come running back to him with tearstained eyes.

When I returned, he always said the same thing. "I forgive you. It's just hormones."

That started me off all over again. "It is not JUST hormones!" I would shout at him. "You don't know anything about hormones, or having babies. If you were nicer to me, I wouldn't have to leave you!"

Once again, it would be the same scenario. Pick up my bags and head for the door. By that time, though, I usually got "that" feeling, not in the pit of my stomach, but higher up. The feeling that it was time to feed the baby...AGAIN.

So I would sit quietly, and wait for the baby to wake up.

Steve would come over and, without saying a word, kiss me gently on the cheek. He knew when it was a good time to be quietly loving.

That, you know, was all that I wanted. I wanted to feel that my husband loved me, even though I was so very fat and flabby. I wanted to feel that he loved me even if I didn't have anything to give back to him at that time. I wanted to feel that he loved me even if I hadn't slept in weeks.

And he showed me that. Because he did love me. His love wasn't conditional, based on my appearance, my sex drive, or cleanliness. And was I happy about that!

29
Challenging Two-Year-Olds

I have a recurring nightmare that I have gone insane and no one notices. I wander around in my dream shouting, and no one thinks it is odd. They just give me that knowing look. "Mom is losing it again. But she'll be fine in a few days."

Then I awaken. As I stumble over strategically placed bits of Lego, I realize there are only two people awake in the house: me, and THE TWO-YEAR-OLD! I know he is awake because I can hear things crashing in the kitchen as he tries to "get it myself."

A two-year-old can bring a mother to her knees before God faster than any force in the universe. The trouble is, he then climbs on her back. It is difficult to pray with a toddler on your back. In fact, it is difficult to pray with a toddler anywhere in the house. As soon as you close your eyes, there is trouble.

Recently, I had a message from a friend. "Terri, I am going OUT OF MY MIND!" That phrase alone clued me in that this must be the work of a two-year-old. My suspicions were indeed confirmed. Her two-year-old had managed, in the space of half an hour, to climb a shelf, dump the contents on herself, tear wallpaper from the wall, color on the couch with permanent marker, and make the baby scream hysterically by taking away his toys. It is no wonder this mom felt that she was going out of her mind.

I called my friend. "Do you want advice, or a shoulder?" I've often found that, when going similarly insane, I wasn't necessarily looking for a "fix." I only wanted someone who would listen to my sob story. As we talked, though, I began to dole out advice to my friend. "Sometimes, the only thing you can do with two-year-olds is keep them with you. Never let them out of your sight. They must be your focus at all times." As I forced my great wisdom upon her, my own two-year-old was sitting nicely on my lap, not getting into trouble in some other place in the house.

But wait! What was that in his hand? A glue stick. He had just glue-sticked (or is it glue-stuck?) his lips together. He thought it was lip balm. And right before my eyes! Perhaps, I thought, I should have stuck to offering my friend a shoulder to sob on.

It's not that I have a low view of the two-year-old child. I adore my little bundle of will. Even in the midst of messes, screaming and hair pulling (mine), of stabbing my feet on plastic soldiers buried in the carpet, God shows me where I can count my blessings.

One such moment occurred when Steve was away at a convention. The children were assembled in the living room for bedtime prayers, but we needed someone to replace Daddy. Bryan, my two-year-old, quickly rose to the task. When it was time for "Daddy" to carry one of the children to bed, he decided he should carry "Bryan." He wrapped Bryan's blanket around his neck, the way Daddy does. Then he carried an imaginary "Bryan" to his bedroom. He carefully laid the nothing down in bed and kissed it goodnight.

I then tried to put my real child into bed. "NO!" he cried. "You'll squish Bryan." He walked importantly to the stairs and said, as his father might, "I'm going to play on the computer now."

Of course, I cannot let my two-year-old play on the computer at nine thirty at night. So I said, " No, Daddy, I think you need to go to bed."

Up he went, and got into MY bed.

A little while later, he came downstairs yelling, "Mom! Mom! Mom!" Two-year-olds can never call you just once.

"Yes, Bryan?"

"I'm not Bryan. I'm Dad."

"Then why did you call me Mom?"

"Oh!" he said. "I have to call you Honey?" Back he went. In a moment, he came running down again. "Honey! There's a monster!"

It's times like those, when our two-year-old sends us to our knees in laughter, that we try to remember in the other times, when we feel we are going insane. If you don't have a two-year-old yourself, stop and pray for someone you know who does. Then offer to baby-sit for an afternoon. The mom will thank you forever.

30
Camp or Hotel?

The twenty-one day trip to California became a reality. I didn't have the best attitude going into the trip. For some reason I had gotten it into my head that I did NOT want to go camping for several days with several children. I needed a vacation, not a lot of extra work.

We began our travels with a twelve-hour drive. We were planning to sleep in the van at a rest stop, but I'm a wimp and don't really enjoy sleeping sitting straight up under the lights of a rest stop. I convinced Steve that it would be better for the *children* to spend the night in a motel.

It is not easy finding a place to sleep to accommodate eight children without spending a fortune. So we spent half a fortune on a suite.

The next morning we arrived at Devil's Tower in Wyoming. We had some fun getting dressed up in those old-fashioned clothes to have our pictures taken. When the owner handed Bryan his rifle he said, "A daddy squirt gun!" He was thrilled, but somehow forgot to smile for the picture.

I began to think I might have problems on our trip when I took Erica into the port-a-potty at a park. She looked down the hole and began to scream hysterically. She then promptly wet her pants. Well, she actually wet my pants.

The second night into our trip we arrived at our first campsite just east of Yellowstone, a place called Bear Creek. As far as the children were concerned, it could have aptly been called "Bears Will Eat You Here" Creek. As soon as we pulled into the campground, John began crying hysterically. He finally managed to sob, "I don't want to be eaten by a bear TONIGHT!" The older girls kept teasing about bears until they had managed to scare themselves. Then, they wouldn't even walk to the bathroom without an adult. I let Steve escort them.

Shortly before going to sleep, we discovered that the previous campers had discarded a watermelon right near the camp. Now that is asking for a bear visitation. Everyone slept that night with one eye open, some because they wanted to see a bear, and some because they didn't want to be eaten. In the morning, we all walked down to the creek, and found real bear tracks. I offered up a prayer of praise that they had stayed by the creek.

We loaded up and headed for Yellowstone. Most of the excitement for us there was the animals. We saw a moose first, just outside the park. It was followed by buffalo crossing the road. A motorcyclist tried to touch one of the buffalo. I told the kids not to watch.

While hiking on a trail at Yellowstone, we encountered a mother bear and her two cubs. Bears don't look quite as scary when they are just sitting down eating berries. Steve and the big kids wanted to continue hiking. I decided to take the little kids the two miles back up the trail. And I mean up!

About halfway up I realized my bad attitude was causing me a lot of real pain. My back was killing me from carrying Bryan and

Erica. I was fat and out of shape and in a terrible mood. That combination does not make for a joyful Mom. In fact, I began feeling that I resembled a mother bear. I may look cute and cuddly, but if you mess with me or one of my little cubs, I will devour you.

Why do you think it is that I could have a bad attitude, know I have a bad attitude, and still keep it? Perhaps, subconsciously, I thought if I made this vacation miserable for everyone, then I would never have to go on a long camping vacation again. Of course, that's not something I could ever admit to anyone.

When we finally reached the top of the mountain, I began to feel an inkling of change. I decided to try to enjoy myself a little more.

My mom used to tell me when I was little, "You are going to do this thing, and you are going to have fun!" Why does her voice always haunt me when I'm being a bad mom?

Singing to the Lord always seems to give me a new lease on life. Which I really needed at that point. So I encouraged everyone to sing.

Driving back later on, we realized that, every time we sang the hymn *As the Deer Panteth For the Water*, a deer appeared. We really wanted to see another moose, so we began singing, "As the moose panteth for the water..." It wasn't effective, and didn't seem to produce the same feeling of worship.

The second night in the tent, I managed to sleep for about two hours. That was progress.

The following day was "geyser day." I overheard a man watching one of these great spouts of water beside us say, "You've seen one geyser, you've seen them all." How is it that the wonders of our creation and our Creator can be looked on as so ordinary?

The following night we camped near a lodge. I gazed longingly at the lodge, knowing that, inside, there were nice bathrooms, a fireplace, and walls.

When we finally arrived in California, Erica went into Grandma's bathroom and said, "Do these toilets flush?" They flushed for the first couple of days anyway. After a session with the plumber and his Roto-Rooter, they flushed once again.

We enjoyed a week there of fun-filled days with family and friends, before leaving the flush toilets and showers again for the "great outdoors."

I purposed in my heart that the trip back was going to be better than the one out. I would be adventurous! I would be fun! I would join the army!

Heading back east, we had a great time playing army through Yosemite. Steve found a couple of walkie-talkies on sale, and decided we should put them to good use. We brushed up on our tracking-the-enemy skills, just in case we might need them some day.

After leaving Yosemite we found ourselves in the middle of nowhere with a nearly empty tank of gas. Every town we went through was closed down for the night. We all prayed that we would not run out of gas. When we finally coasted into an open gas station, everyone shouted, "Hallelujah!" It was neat to see the provision of the Lord in such a tangible way. I knew the Lord's provision with my attitude was also worth a shout of "Hallelujah!"

That night, unable to find a campground, we stayed in a refurbished 1800s motel. The toilet was the kind with a box up on the wall and a pull string. It was quite interesting, but still scary for our four-year-old.

The next few days we spent camping, and viewing some of the most marvelous, breathtaking sights I had ever seen.

At the Grand Canyon, I told the children about the time their dad and I were there during an electrical storm. When I waved my arm through the air, I could see light following my hand. When Steve reached for my arm, he got a shocking experience!

As we trooped out to a point with the kids, we could see each other's hair sticking straight up. The feel of electricity in the air frightened some of the kids.

You can't see the Grand Canyon and not take a photo. Even if the clouds *are* threatening to dump massive amounts of water on you. I lined everyone up at the edge and whispered, "Smile."

Together, they counted, "One...Two...Three Electricity!" They all yelled in unison, creating beautiful smiles on every one of their faces. It produced a roar of laughter from the crowd that had assembled to watch eight kids get their picture taken in the midst of a storm.

By the third consecutive night of camping, I was plain sick of it. Steve sent me alone on the mile-long hike to the registration area. Someone knew that I needed a little "alone" time. I cried as I walked. The last thing I wanted to do was spend one more night on hard ground. Even when I paid the money for our site, I was still hoping that Steve would change his mind and get us a motel room for the night.

As I walked back toward the tent, though, something miraculous happened. I was the one who had a change of heart. My attitude was the one that needed an adjustment, not Steve's. As I complained to the Lord about how awful it was to have to spend all this time in a tent, He gently reminded me what a blessing it is for me to have such a wonderful family. I'm always complaining at home about not doing anything fun. And here I was without any cleaning responsibilities, being a grouch.

I rounded a corner and saw with a clearer vision the responsibility I had to the children and to Steve, to help create memories that will stay with us for a lifetime. I felt the tears dry up as a smile began to form on my face.

I thought of how much Steve loves to camp. I began to wonder if making an effort to enjoy something I hated might be an issue of submission for me. There was still time to pray before I arrived back at the campsite. I asked the Lord to help me to be the wife that He wants me to be, even if it meant I had to spend a few more nights in a tent on hard ground.

Later that night, we had a good time playing a game with the older kids while the little ones slept in the tent. When I kissed Steve goodnight there was a smile on my face instead of a frown.

The following morning we started out on what is arguably the most scenic highway in the U.S., leaving Bryce Canyon and heading toward Colorado. We took a small highway, soaking up the wonders of God's creation as the mountains and the forests merged into tremendous splendor.

That night we ended up in a motel! We swam in the pool, sat in the hot tub, took hot baths and showers, and even slept in clean beds. I refused to allow anyone entrance into the bed without first having washed the sand and dirt off their feet. I did not want gravel in my toes that night.

The next morning, Steve took a poll, and we voted to go home. So we drove for fifteen hours, arriving home late that night. During the drive, Steve talked about our next camping trip. Next year.

I thought, "At least it's a year away."

I'm thinking that, if I change my name to Terri Hotel by next year, then I don't have to go camping.

Of course if I changed my name to Terri Hotel, I wouldn't have people asking me if I'm married to Steve Camp.

I am married to Steve Camp. But not the singer. I'm married to Steve Camp the totally awesome dude, who on many occasions has put up with me being a raving lunatic.

31
When Did I Get Fat?

Giving birth to my son Bryan took quite a toll on my body. I was told to rest for several weeks. And, at first, I needed to. Everything I did seemed to be too much. So I rested. And I rested.

I liked resting. I began spending more time resting at my computer. I stopped taking the kids outside for walks and play.

Before I knew it, I had rested myself into about twenty extra pounds. Two and a half years after Bryan was born, I weighed only five pounds less than I did when I gave birth to him.

This came home to me when we went on our vacation to California.

Part of the reason for the trip was so that Steve could attend his twentieth high school reunion. I didn't know anyone there, so mostly I just engaged in one of my favorite pastimes, people watching.

Usually, I enjoy interpreting body language, observing how people talk and behave. However, during the reunion we were seated directly across from a woman who must have spent seven hours a day in a gym for the last twenty years. Of course, I consoled myself, she didn't have eight children.

But next to her was a woman who had six children, and she looked almost as fit as her friend. I started thinking horrible things about them, because they wasted all of their time at a gym. All I was doing was avoiding the truth: that I had let myself go to pot! And my poor husband had to look at me every day.

When Steve and I were married, I was tiny. I didn't gain much weight with my first few children. But after Bryan was born, I didn't take any of it off.

Steve got used to me undressing in the dark. And I got used to jumping quickly into bed, before the moonlight revealed to him how truly lumpy I had become.

I became obsessed about the way I looked. I avoided looking in the mirror. I even angled the mirror in my bedroom so that it would make me look taller and slimmer. It was an illusion, but one that I was willing to put up with so I could at least make sure my clothes matched.

I used to stare into mirrors and smile at myself. I once heard that, if you smile at yourself, it will make you smile back. But the smile was followed now with a frown. I began to imagine that Steve was looking at other women. I know he wasn't, but I imagined that he was.

I kept thinking that all my old friends were sitting around saying, "Boy, Terri got fat!" As I sat at the reunion, I vowed that I was going to make some changes.

But how? Going to a gym was not an option. There aren't a lot of gyms scattered in the cornfields of Iowa. From where we lived, it would take me nearly an hour to get to one.

I felt myself sink further into despair.

I decided that, if I really wanted to change how I looked, I would have to change my whole lifestyle. I would have to evaluate, honestly, all that I had been doing to get myself to this point.

I knew that I didn't want to go on some fad diet, losing weight and then gaining it right back in the next few months. So, researching to find the perfect diet for me soon became an obsession. I didn't want it to be painful. I wanted it to be fast. But I didn't want a fad diet. Well, there wasn't anything like that.

I learned a lot about all the diets out there. Low carbohydrate and high protein. High carbohydrate and low protein. For every "perfect" diet, there is an opposite "perfect" diet.

Finally, I did the right thing. I went to the Lord.

I had to go to Him, because I was obsessed about this weight thing. He was the only one who was going to cure me. And help me get on the path that I wanted to be on.

He led me to make several resolutions. First, there was my Pepsi habit. I always had a Pepsi with me. I decided that the habit had to go, once and for all. An occasional drink, when I really wanted it, was fine. I didn't want this resolution to make me feel like a slave to what I ate or drank.

Steve had been after me for years to drink more water. When I told him of my desire to quit drinking Pepsi and begin drinking water, he went out and bought a filter for our water. Wasn't that extremely kind of him? He didn't see why I was so worked up about the weight thing, but he wanted to do anything he could to help me.

He even allowed me to get a treadmill for the house. I wanted to start exercising every day, but didn't feel that getting outside for a walk would always be feasible. Our winters are too harsh. But I knew that, if I didn't keep at it consistently, I would drop the exercise completely.

The first day of water only, and walking on the treadmill, was horrendous. I developed an appalling headache from caffeine withdrawal, and could only manage to walk for ten minutes. I felt defeated.

But I had resolved that I was going to turn my life around. So I continued to plug away.

I discovered, through my resolution, that eating more than one cookie at a time wasn't as appealing if I imagined it adding bulk to my body. So I learned to go without the second one.

I also learned what a mistake it is to put your body into starvation mode. This was the way I had lived, and I couldn't understand how I got so fat when I barely ate any food. It was because my body wasn't getting the fuel it needed to keep me going, so I rested instead of working out.

There have been a few pitfalls along the way in the months since I made my resolve to slim down and get into shape. But, for the most part, I have felt successful. With the Lord's help, I have changed into a healthier, more vibrant, and more active person.

And Steve really likes it!

32
Time for the Lord

While I began to shrink away my fat cells, I heard a small quiet voice say to me, "Why aren't you so diligent about your time with me?"

GULP.

Sure enough, I had been able to set aside an hour every day to work off my fat cells. But my whole life I had struggled with being able to find adequate time to spend with the Lord.

I had tried getting up before everyone else, but that didn't work. My kids sleep in late, except if they hear that someone else is up. I tried staying in my room, but I often snuggled under the covers to stay warm, and found myself waking up an hour later, Bible open on my lap, pen poised to write, and nothing on the paper or in my heart.

With eight children in the house, I didn't even attempt to try to spend time alone with the Lord during the day. The children always know where Mom is. I always ended up telling eight different people not to interrupt me. I could not bring myself simply to shout, "LEAVE ME ALONE!"

So there I was, knowing that my relationship with the Lord needed to be nurtured. Knowing that I needed to make it a priority in my life. And not knowing how to do it.

I decided to extend my exercise time to allow time to spend with the Lord. I decided that I could walk on the treadmill and listen to praise music.

Any of my children will tell you that Mom is dripping wet when she's finished her treading. I like to take a hot bath after my workout, as I lovingly refer to it. So, why not extend the bath a bit longer and spend the whole time with the Lord?

The first day of my new schedule, I entered the hot bath, excited to spend some quality time with the Lord.

I began my prayer. "Dear Lord,"

A knock on the bathroom door. "Mom, John's not cleaning!"

I heaved a sigh as I told David to have John come to the door. "Put all your clothes away," I told him.

Then I heard, "Bryan, stop that!"

So I had to call Bryan to the door. He said, "Erica is being mean."

I called Erica to the door.

Finally all was quiet. I began where I left off. "Dear Lord"

Another knock. "Mom, the phone is for you." Did they really think I was going to get out of the tub to answer it?

"I'll call back later," I said, through the door. "Who is it?"

It was a dear friend I hadn't talked to in ages. "Wait!" I cried. "I'll get out."

I spent the next forty minutes in the tub conversing with my friend, not with the Lord as I had intended.

I felt awful about it.

I sat in my cold bathwater and talked with the Lord. I started whining about my inability to be able to draw near to Him when I want to. But then, the Lord reminded me that I can draw near to

Him all the time. I can take Him in the car with me. I can get up with Him. I can even be with Him while I'm vacuuming the living room. He didn't require me to stop all that I do, just to do it with Him.

Jesus wants me to walk with Him continually. When I get on the floor to play trains with one of my little ones, Jesus wants to be with me. When I read aloud to all the kids, Jesus wants to be there, too. When I get a moment when all the children are busy in their own little worlds, He wants to be with me. If I keep Him always with me, then my priorities will be right. My focus will be on Him and not on things. I will then truly be living the passage in Deuteronomy 6 with my children: "And these words which I command you today shall be in your heart. You shall teach them diligently to your children, and shall talk of them when you sit in your house, when you walk by the way, when you lie down and when you rise up" (Deut. 6:6,7).

When I allow Jesus to walk through my life with me, then He will also be walking with my children.

There is no greater joy than to know that Jesus is walking with my children. And that my children are walking with Him.

33
And What Is It YOU Do?

I always knew that I wanted to be a stay-at-home mom. I was determined that I would be the BEST stay-at-home mom ever.

When I was first married, I still had a career woman mentality. I resigned from the Air Force only a week before Ashley was born. But I loved taking care of my new baby.

I was fairly solid in my conviction to stay home with my children. However, shortly after our second child, Christi, was born, we went through a tough time financially. I had become a Christian by then, so I asked the Lord to guide me to a job. I applied everywhere. I even applied at a newly built warehouse store, where the only people who weren't hired were total losers.

I didn't get the job.

My trust remained strong in the Lord. I took this as a sign that He wanted me to stay at home with my children.

About a week later, Steve received a promotion and a raise. Two weeks after that, he received a second promotion, and another raise. We were able to pay all our bills, and still had enough left to buy food.

I didn't think of working anymore.

Not too long after that time, home computers began to appear on the market. We bought a computer for Christmas. Steve knew that my passion in life was writing, and he hoped that I would use the computer for that purpose. For years, I had filled page after page of lined paper. Now, he often commented that, if I could only get it published, then life would be great!

Well, we did a lot with that computer. We played games on it. Mostly solitaire. A deck of cards would have been a lot cheaper.

As our family grew, and we began to homeschool the children, the opportunity presented itself for me to write regularly for a homeschool newsletter. Six years after the fact, I was finally using the computer for its intended purpose. It felt good to sit down and write on a regular basis, even though I wasn't making money. The kids all knew when it was newsletter-writing time. I plopped them down in front of the TV all day, and hid myself in my room to put the newsletter together. I loved it.

Then, my first article was published. Wow! Again, no paycheck, but I was thrilled. As the years passed, I found myself writing more. Along with that came the new thrill of speaking to groups of other mothers who were homeschooling.

Through all that, I remained faithful to my first calling as a stay-at-home, homeschooling mom.

Then my first book was published. And my second book was available for sale. Invitations to speak came more often. I spoke with increasing frequency at conferences and Mom's Night Out meetings. Was it fun! I was almost on a high from it.

People began to tell me that I was getting famous.

As much as I tried to keep my life the same, it began to change. I began to look for opportunities to go out speaking. I wanted to take the children with me, but that wasn't an option most of the time.

The struggle had begun. I was enjoying the thought of being a career woman. I started feeling that the "ministry" God had called me to was more important than the mundane tasks of motherhood.

I could not seem to find the balance I so desperately wanted.

One night, I felt an especially heavy weight of failure in my place as mother and wife. We were gathered to pray with the children, and, as I bowed my head, Steve began, "Dear Lord, please help Mommy—" I was certain he was going to ask that the Lord help me to be a better mother. Instead, he said: "You have given her a ministry outside our home. She is struggling with balance in her life. Lord, please help all of us to help her with the tasks at home, to make it easier for her to do the ministry you have called her to."

I was floored! He seemed to value what I was doing. He wanted me to put more effort into that ministry. He even wanted the kids to know it was important.

But, whenever I mentioned another opportunity to leave our house, Steve was less encouraging. He began to complain that I was always gone. And I began to feel angry.

As I searched for balance in my life, I realized the problem wasn't that I was always gone. The problem was that I wanted to be gone. I found that, coming home after a few days away, I secretly wished that I had another place to go. Things at home could run smoothly without me. Why, I reasoned, did I have to be there? Ashley was capable of homeschooling the other children.

Balance didn't need to come from rearranging my time, but my attitude. I needed to want to be home, even when I was called away.

The change came when I had to be gone, not for anything so glamorous as a speaking engagement, but to help my mom through surgery. As I was preparing to leave, I realized I didn't want to go. During the six hours' drive to my mom's place, all

I thought about was my children and my husband at home. I knew they were in good hands. It wasn't that I worried about them. I just wanted to be with them.

I thought of my family often while I was away. When I arrived back home, I felt that the Lord had changed my heart.

Still I struggled. Thoughts drifted through my head that being a wife and a mom wasn't enough. I even began toying with the idea of going back to school. "Hey," I told myself, "I could go to college, then to law school." I had dreamed of being a lawyer when I was sixteen.

What did that have to do with my life now?

Finally, one night, I said to Steve, "I've been struggling with the idea of having a career."

To which he said, "Well, stop it!"

I laughed to myself. But I realized that he was right. What did I think a career would do for me? Would it make people respect me? Would they walk by and say, "Hey, there's a great career woman"? As I thought about this, I realized how ridiculous the whole idea was.

Why would I want to go to college, just so that I could go out to work day after day? I would rather stay home with my children. I have the best career in the world.

Besides, it's fun to sit across from someone at a banquet and watch her face when I say, for the second time, "Yes, I really do have eight children." And I don't feel any need to add, "And I write books, and I speak at conferences, and here is a list of my accomplishments."

The next time someone says to me, "And what is it you do?" I will get a little taller as I tell them, "I'm a wife and a mom!"

Conclusion: The Perfect Wife

It was a weekend that would go down in history as the time when everything went wrong. So many little things went wrong, problems that, in sufficient numbers, can reduce mere mortals to raving lunatics. I, being a perfect wife, held on to my composure through it all and said to my husband, "Will you please fix everything!"

It began Friday morning. I was heading out to the post office when I noticed that the heater fan in my car was not working. I drove the thirty miles shivering in subfreezing temperatures.

When I returned home, I did what all perfect wives do. I telephoned Steve. He walked me through a couple of ideas, checking the fuses, looking at the belts. Nothing worked.

Since I had to go out again, I took the van. Returning home, I began to back into the parking spot next to the electrical outlet, so that I could plug in the engine. Suddenly, the tires were spinning out on a sheet of ice. We were not going anywhere but round in circles.

By this time, Steve was home. So I did what all perfect wives do. I went in and asked him to move the van.

He was in the middle of trying to fix his computer, which had fried the night before. He said he would try to get the van unstuck if I would take over working on the computer. Which I did.

The van wouldn't start.

I continued working on his computer. Nothing happened, except that I seemed to be getting chilled. I checked to see if I had a fever. No. So I checked the thermostat. The temperature in the house was falling.

I went to the basement to see if one of my little switch monsters had flipped off the furnace switch. The switch was on, but there was no sound from the heater. Not really expecting much, I flipped the switch off, then on again.

It worked! The house would only take a few hours to warm back up.

Normally, so many things going wrong at once would send me into a tizzy. I like to be in control. I like everything to work according to my plan. And my plan requires that things work perfectly, or nearly so.

We had made plans to go away for the weekend, but those were thwarted by the weather. So I did what all perfect women do when they cannot control a situation. I decided to take a hot bath.

When I stepped into the water, I noticed right away that it didn't feel right. That's when I was reminded of what Steve had said when I came in after getting the van stuck on ice. "The toilet has been running for hours. We won't have any soft water for a few days."

That didn't register as a big deal until I wanted to take a bath. Now, I needed that problem fixed too.

Still, and surprisingly, I managed to remain in a fairly good mood through the piling up of these irritations.

After we had all the children tucked in for the night, Steve and I relaxed with our respective electronic entertainments. Then, the house lights flickered off and on.

I was working on this book. The chapter I was writing is now gone forever. Oh well, it probably wasn't that good anyway.

Steve quickly fetched his flashlight, just in case it happened again and he needed to rescue me in the dark. Then he went looking for one for me.

He had to try four flashlights before he found one that worked. He gave it to me, and I settled back down to my computer.

The lights went out again. I sat there for quite awhile, staring in the dark at a dead computer.

Finally, I turned on my flashlight hoping that if I turned on the flashlight it would somehow prompt my computer to work. It did not. So I followed Steve to the door. He went out into the blizzard to see if one of our wires had come down. While he was out there, and just for fun, he tried again to get the van going. This time, it started.

Earlier in the evening, I had taken out an extension cord so that I could plug it in from where it was stuck. Now, I was thankful for my quick thinking.

It had only taken me twenty-four hours to think of it.

Steve came in smiling. Well, at least in the morning we would be able to get the van started. We might not be able to move it, but we would pile all the kids into it anyway, ready to go to church.

We sat up for a few minutes longer, waiting for the lights to come back on. We even joked about how interesting it was that so many things were going wrong around our house.

At one fifteen, still in the dark, we went to bed.

You may wonder what all this has to do with being the perfect wife. I'm getting to that.

Eve was created to be the perfect companion for Adam. Of course, nothing went wrong in the garden until Eve ate the fruit. Up until that point, there weren't any household maintenance problems. They never had to worry about getting the camel started in the morning.

But then she messed everything up, by giving in to the crafty dude.

Is there any way we can get back to that place of perfection, when sin abounds in the world and things go wrong more often than not?

Many of us simply say, "Well, we live in a fallen world. There is nothing we can do about it, so let's just live it up!"

I don't believe that is the answer.

I think the answer lies in understanding what God was doing when He created Eve. Why did He create her for man?

He created her because man was alone. But wait a minute! Man wasn't alone. He had God. And he had the animals. But God saw that man needed someone to help him. Someone who would be comparable to him, a companion. Someone to help him tend the garden.

I often forget that I am here to help my husband. Instead, I find myself thinking that he is here to be my hero. He is here to make sure that everything in the house is in proper working order. And if I am in a bad mood, I think it's his responsibility to change my attitude.

When Eve listened to the serpent, she landed all of us women after her with an attitude—not to mention the laundry, the dirty dishes, and pain in childbirth. Because of Eve's sin, I cannot be a perfect person now, on earth. But I can still strive to be a perfect wife. As long as I know that being a perfect wife does not mean I will never sin.

I still don't do laundry. I still don't do dishes. And I can't have any more children. So what does make a perfect wife?

A perfect wife is a helper comparable to her husband. A perfect wife remembers to plug in the van when it's minus thirty outside. A perfect wife makes spaghetti for dinner, just because her husband likes it.

A perfect wife looks at her husband every day, and says, "Thank you, Lord!"

Also by Terri:

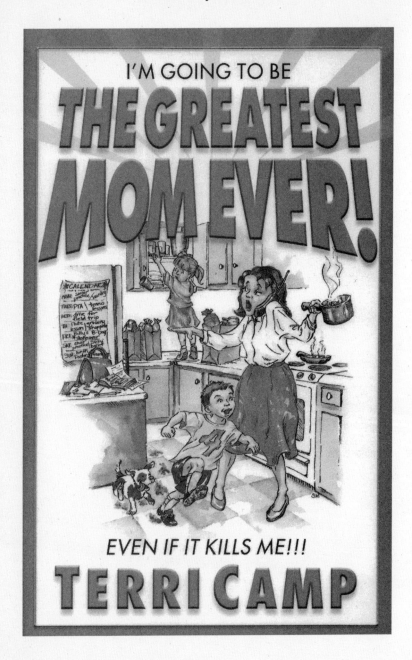

I'M GOING TO BE
THE GREATEST
MOM EVER!

EVEN IF IT KILLS ME!!!

TERRI CAMP

ISBN: 1-929125-08-9 $10.99

YOU'RE JUST ONE CLICK AWAY FROM GREATNESS.

 Loyal Publishing: *Faithful to the Word.*

ABOUT	PRODUCTS	AUTHORS	RESELLERS	STORE

By logging on to loyalpublishing.com, you can find out how to hear Terri in person, send her a note, or purchase products that are only available from Loyal.

Also From Loyal:

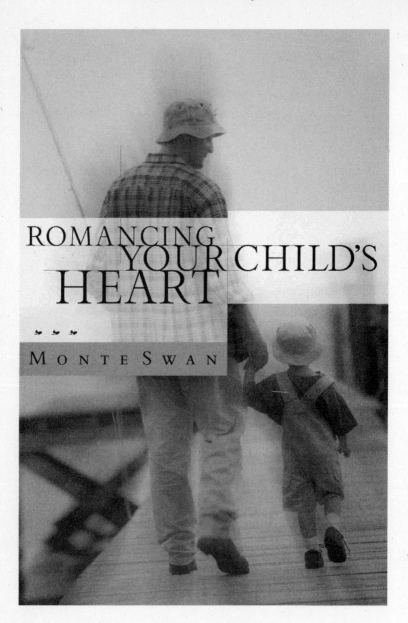

ROMANCING
YOUR CHILD'S
HEART

M O N T E S W A N

ISBN: 1-929125-16-X $12.99